Essentials
For Catholic Teens

Edited by Lewis Dowle

Nihil Obstat: Rt. Rev. Bishop Mark O'Toole
Bishop of Plymouth, United Kingdom, 04/04/17.

The Nihil Obstat is an official declaration that a book is
free of doctrinal or moral error and that ecclesiastical
permission for its publication has been granted.

DEDICATION

To all Catholic youth in the world. You are the Saints not just of tomorrow, but also today.

"Let no one despise your youth, but set the believers an example in speech and conduct, in love, in faith, in purity" (1 Timothy 4:12).

With so many challenges for young people, they need the fuel to stand for Christ and run the race. In "Essentials for Catholic Teens", it encourages young Catholics to live life to the full in Christ (John 10:10).

The Holy Spirit leaps off the pages and is a great resource for all young people. We highly recommend this book to all Catholic teens.

Mario & Anna Cappello, Founders of the ICPE Mission.

If only I had this book when I was 15. Now at 67, and with the "experience" of age I realise what I have missed! It is packed with a series of personal journeys to better know and love Our Lord and Saviour Jesus Christ. The guidance is illustrated with Scripture, the Catechism, sayings of the Saints and grounded by the personal life encounters of the varied young contributors. These writers know Jesus and want you to get to know Him too, as your personal Best Friend.

If you want to grow in faith "to be the saint God is calling you to be", then read this book! It is the road map to life on fire with the Holy Spirit! It should be required reading for all young people in our parishes and schools. It is the "New Evangelism" for the young, and for all it is confirmation that: "we are what he has made us, created in Christ Jesus for good works, which God prepared beforehand to be our way of life" (page 192, Ephesians 2:10).

I thank Jesus for all the writers, their supporters and families. I pray for all our young people, that the Holy Spirit will lead them to read, and see their Father's Love Letter to them, revealed by this book.

Deacon Andrew Shute, Our Lady of the Portal and St Piran, Truro.

This book is a collection of individuals and their journey with God. This is not a theological exegesis but Catholics sharing their everyday walk with God and what they are learning along the way.

ACKNOWLEDGMENTS

This book has been a blessing with the help and support of many people. To each and every author of this book, thank you. It wouldn't have been possible without you. Thank you to each of the anonymous young people who contributed a testimony as well. The support and hard work of Mia Swientek is greatly appreciated. Thank you also to Brian Suhada and Will Desmond. Thank you to Mario and Anna Cappello with their 'Yes' to God with the ICPE Mission. I will always be grateful to ICPE.

Thank you to Charles Whitehead for your belief and support of young people. To Team Jehu, Team Middlewick and Team Buscombe, thank you for your support with the youth ministry. I am hugely grateful to Mary for her time and work for the book. Thank you also to Mark and Pat Dol for the privilege to serve in youth ministry with you. A huge thank you as well to Bishop Mark and his amazing support; I am so grateful. Finally, thank you to my family: you are the best and this book would not have been possible without your support.

Lewis Dowle <><

CONTENTS

FOREWORD I – BISHOP MARK O'TOOLE

I was delighted to see this publication of "Essentials for Catholic Teens" and highly recommend it. It has been a joy to read the text and to realise what an impact this will make on many young people seeking Christ in His Church. Lewis Dowle and his young co-authors put before us their own faith in Jesus and the fullness of life that they have found in Him. In doing so, they make a refreshing contribution to the call for a New Evangelisation, expressing a "new ardour" for the Gospel and what Jesus teaches us about being fully human. This is especially true of those for whom this book is produced and dedicated, the young of the world, who are called to be the saints of today.

There is no better tool for evangelisation than having the courage to witness to others and to talk naturally with them about our personal encounter with the Lord. Although the book is aimed at teenagers, and will certainly encourage them in deepening and talking about their faith, it will surely inspire people of all ages. The authors speak to us in humility but with a confidence and courage which is often lacking in our own Christian discipleship. Their use of personal experiences and "story" echo that of the Master Himself.

I am sure you will enjoy reading the different reflections in the book and I know it will repay your time and attention a hundredfold. May many be brought to a deeper encounter with Jesus in His Church through it, and may each of us develop the courage of these young disciples to bear witness to Jesus with enthusiasm and energy.

+ Rt Rev Mark O'Toole

Bishop of Plymouth, United Kingdom.
Chair of the Catholic Bishop's Department
of Evangelisation and Catechesis.

FOREWORD II – CHARLES WHITEHEAD

I have known Lewis Dowle for several years and it has been a source of great pleasure to watch him grow into a mature and committed young Christian leader. I was unaware, however, that he possessed a gift for writing, so it was a great joy to receive a draft copy of **"Essentials for Catholic Teens"** which he has co-authored and edited, with a request to write the foreword which I'm delighted to accept.

This is an excellent and stimulating book which my wife Sue and I both thoroughly enjoyed reading, and we feel sure that the very modern approach taken to explaining the Catholic faith will make it appealing and extremely helpful to a host of teenage readers. It is aimed primarily at a 13 to 16 year old teenage readership, and I am sure it will lead them deeper in their relationship with God and get them excited about their faith. Master-minded and brought together by Lewis, the fifteen chapters draw on the experience and wisdom of a number of other gifted young Catholic writers from four different continents, all clearly on fire in their faith.

So I have no hesitation in recommending this very contemporary book for the remarkable ways in which it brings many of the eternal truths of our faith alive in new, exciting and memorable ways.

"Essentials for Catholic Teens" deals very comprehensively with all the main areas of Catholic faith and practice, and the fact that the author of each chapter is clearly doing his or her best to faithfully live out the truth contained in their particular topic ensures that the reader is kept both interested and challenged. The book explains pretty well everything a teenage Catholic will be questioning and needs to understand - **Salvation, Prayer, the Bible, Worship, Thanksgiving, the Eucharist, the Rosary, Theology of the Body, Reconciliation, Sainthood and more**, with frequent references to the Catechism, YOUCAT, Church documents and the wisdom of several Popes. Complex truths are addressed in a straight-forward, easy to understand way, always a great blessing to any reader - thank you, Lewis.

The final part of the book consists of a number of very different and stimulating testimonies from a variety of young people. In the introduction to this closing section we are reminded: **"Whether it is a 'big or small' conversion, each of our stories are important to God and will speak to people"**. I am convinced that "Essentials for Catholic Teens" is important to God, and will speak very powerfully to all those who read it, just as it has to me.

Charles Whitehead

Chairman of the International Charismatic Consultation (ICC),
Director of Premier Christian Radio,
and Founder of Celebrate Catholic Conference.

CHAPTER 1: SALVATION'S STORY
Lewis Dowle

When he isn't outdoors exploring, Lewis is a student at university in the UK. He enjoys seeing young people getting excited about God. Outside of studying he loves music, playing football, and minions.

Expeditions

We're about to set out on a very exciting voyage. It is going to be an expedition across lands we know, and lands we've not yet chartered. For this adventure that we're on, we will need to make sure we have everything we need before we set out, this is our water, food and GPS. For every mission, you need the brief, the background of where we're coming from, where we fit into it, and where we're going. So let's kick it off!

In the beginning before the universe ever existed, God lived. He is begotten, not created, that means that nothing and no one made Him because He is God. God is one God but three persons, the Trinity of Father, Son and Holy Spirit. In the creation of the world God said, "Let us make humankind in our image, according to our likeness" (Genesis 1:26). And so we were made.

But our first parents didn't follow God, they instead listened to the serpent, the devil. They wanted to be like God and the devil lied to them that if they ate of the tree of the

Knowledge of Good and Evil they would become like God. The devil had tricked them. Because of this, sin came into the world and sin is very serious. It separated us from God.

But God wanted us. Desperately. So He came up with a plan. A way for us to be in Communion with God again. And the plan? You guessed it, Jesus! God's only Son. **It's kinda amazing when you think about it how God so loved us that He sent His only Son to die for us (John 3:16)!** Not only that, God had spoken to His people through the prophets in the Old Testament saying how a Messiah was coming. God had planned it all. The thing is though, Jesus wasn't born in a palace like some thought He would be, and He wasn't the rich and powerful warrior they were expecting. **But our God is full of surprises.**

Jesus was born in a stable, hardly the birthplace of a King, but from the word go Jesus shows us humility. The prophets foretold that a virgin would have a child, that the child would be born in Bethlehem, and, lo and behold, that's what happened. Mary, a teen just like you was told by an angel called Gabriel that she would have a child who would be...well God. But born as a human, and born *of* a human. **You see when Jesus came into the world He was both fully human and fully divine.** Both God *and* man. Jesus is that bridge, He came to restore our friendship with God.

So this girl of about 14 years old was told she would have a child. Only the thing is she wasn't married. But she was engaged. Now this is an awkward moment. Her fiancé Joseph would surely find out that Mary was pregnant, and then what would she say? As you can imagine Mary was probably just a little taken aback by the angel Gabriel's words, but Mary simply said, "Let it be with according to your word" (Luke 1:38). In Mary's simple 'yes' to God, the face of the earth was changed forever. **For-ever.** Jesus was coming into our world, and He was coming to save His people, and that is what His Name means, as "he will save his people from their sins" (Matthew 1:21). You and I. Jesus came for *us*.

"But God proves his love for us in that while we still were sinners Christ died for us" (Romans 5:8).

The thing is, we had walked away from God because our first parents Adam and Eve rejected God. Their first sin, their original sin, was passed down to all of us. We had sinned and that sin needed to be dealt with as it was keeping us from God. The sin needed to be paid for and this is the coolest part: **Christ paid the price.**

So after Mary had said yes to being the mother of God, the Holy Family of St Joseph, Mary and Jesus lived happily together. Jesus lived a normal life like you and I. He would have been a carpenter most likely, like Joseph. When He reached the age of 30 though, **all heaven breaks loose.** Jesus started to preach. He would say 'Come' and people would come. In the Gospel of Mark, one of the very first words from Jesus is this word 'Come'. It's an invitation to you and I. We are invited. We are *called*. Jesus is inviting us into a relationship. Pope Francis said:

> "The Lord is knocking at the door of our
> hearts. Have we put a sign on the door
> saying: 'Do not disturb'?"

And it is exactly that: will we open the door to Him?

God calls us friends. And the cool thing is this: it is because of Jesus. We don't have to earn that title. He doesn't stop at friends either. God goes on to call us His children... and even heirs (Galatians 4:7)!

Jesus' mission on earth was to spread His teachings, His mercy and His love; He showed us how to live. He spoke on everything you can imagine. Not only that, He worked miracles. **Big** miracles. From telling the storm and oceans to be still, to calling Lazarus up from the sleep of death. He came not for the really good people any more than the slightly unusual people. In fact Jesus came for sinners (1 Timothy 1:15), and just as a doctor comes to help the sick rather than the healthy, so Jesus came for us (Mark 2:17).

So what happened next? We call this the Passion of Christ. This is how Jesus gave Himself over to be crucified on a cross for us out of love. He died for us so that we could have life and to show us how much He loves us. As the saying goes, 'actions speak louder than words', what greater action could Jesus do to show us that He loves us than to give His life for us.

"No one has greater love than this, to lay
down one's life for one's friends"
(John 15:13)

Jesus was betrayed by Judas, handed over to the chief priests and Pharisees who brought Him before Pilate. Jesus' disciples deserted Him, and even His own people (the Jews) shouted before Pilate for Jesus to be crucified on the cross, the most brutal form of death and punishment the Roman Empire knew. **And Jesus knew all that was about to happen.** He knew the pain He would endure. He knew He would be whipped, mocked, spat on, insulted, jeered at and rejected. He knew He would be nailed to a cross, He knew He didn't deserve it. Jesus had all the power to come down from the cross, but He didn't. And why? Because as He was on the cross, He was thinking about you. Jesus couldn't get you out of His mind. And He knew the only way we could spend forever with Him was if He died for our sins. And He did just that.

But with Jesus, death is never the end. Three days after Jesus' death we come to the greatest celebration in the Church: **the Resurrection!** The Church says this:

Dying you destroyed our death
Rising you restored out life
Lord Jesus, come in glory

Jesus rose from the dead, completing His mission on earth to destroy sin and restore us! But Jesus' role doesn't end here. After His Resurrection He appeared to more than 500 people (1 Corinthians 5:6). Jesus even walked through walls to see the disciples (John 20:19; Luke 24:36). On seeing them He issued them the instruction to stay where they were in Jerusalem and wait for the Holy Spirit to come (Luke 24:49). He said how just as God had sent Him, so He is sending you and I into the world.

Just as Jesus said, so the disciples did. We can read about this cool story in the book of Acts.

> "When the day of Pentecost had come, they were all together in one place. And suddenly from heaven there came a sound like the rushing of a violent wind, and it filled the entire house where they were sitting. Divided tongues, as of fire, appeared among them, and a tongue rested on each of them. All of them were filled with the Holy Spirit..."
> (Acts 2:1-4).

The Holy Spirit came on each of the disciples, and if we read on, the people thought that the disciples were drunk because they were all so happy, speaking different languages! But what or who is the Holy Spirit? Soul Survivor (a church in the UK) said how Jesus is called Emmanuel which means "God-with-us", and the Holy Spirit is "God-**in**-us". The Holy Spirit lives in each of us as Christians, when we are baptised or give our lives to Jesus, His Holy Spirit comes upon us and fills us with some incredible things. In St Paul's letter to the Galatians (Gal 5:22-23), he writes that the fruits of the spirit, i.e. the outcomes of being a Christian are these:

- Love
- Joy
- Peace
- Patience
- Kindness
- Generosity
- Faithfulness
- Gentleness
- Self-control

Just as these fruits (no relation to fruit salads) are God's gifts to us and signs of His presence in each of us, so too are they characteristics of God Himself. He is love. He is kind. He is faithful. But God's Holy Spirit is much more than just this. As He went to be with the Father, He didn't leave us alone. His Holy Spirit is the promise of Jesus. With the Holy Spirit we are never alone, He is with us always.

"And I will ask the Father, and he will give you another Advocate [Helper], to be with you forever. This is the Spirit of truth, whom the world cannot receive, because it neither sees him nor knows him. You know him, because he abides with you, and he will be in you" (John 14:16-17).

This is God alive in us. He is in heaven, and He is in us. And He has equipped us. Just as an army general would equip his army, so too has God equipped us with all the weapons and armour that we need for battle (check out Chapters 5 and 8). Jesus said to His disciples:

"Very truly, I tell you, the one who believes in me will also do the works that I do and, in fact, will do greater works than these, because I am going to the Father" (John 14:12).

And what did Jesus do? He raised people from the dead. He healed the blind. He turned water into wine. He walked on water. He spoke to the storms and they stilled. So Jesus did these amazing miracles, and yet He says we will do 'even greater works'? How can this be so? Because of the Holy Spirit. The book of Acts is all about this. The apostles who were once scared, were now brave. Those who were afraid were know standing up for Christ even if it meant death. St Paul knew the power of Holy Spirit and wrote all about the miracles of God. **But what we must realise is this: the same Holy Spirit is alive in us.**

"I pray that the God of our Lord Jesus Christ, the Father of glory, may give you a spirit of wisdom and revelation as you

> come to know him, so that, with the eyes
> of your heart enlightened, you may know
> what is the hope to which he has called
> you, what are the riches of his glorious
> inheritance among the saints, and what is
> the immeasurable greatness of his power
> for us who believe, according to the
> working of his great power. God put this
> power to work in Christ when he raised
> him from the dead and seated him at his
> right hand in the heavenly places"
> (Ephesians 1:17-20).

This means that we have been given gifts. But as the wise philosopher (Spiderman) would say, with great power comes great responsibility. These gifts have been given with a purpose. For the glory of God. We have been given gifts to build each other up, to lead others to God, and to grow in holiness.

And that's where this book comes into play...

CHAPTER 2: SECRET STRENGTH – THANKSGIVING
Isabella Toth

Isabella is a Theology graduate with a love for Scripture, especially in its original languages! She enjoys being outdoors in God's creation and is currently training to be an accountant. She keeps chickens in her garden which produce fresh eggs each day which provides a great excuse for her to keep baking cakes!

"Joy is the gigantic secret of the Christian"
(G.K. Chesterton)

Saying "thank you" is something we are taught to do from a young age, but do you know that giving thanks to God can really transform your relationship with Him and the way you see life?

"O give thanks to the LORD for he is good; for his steadfast love endures forever" (Psalm 106:1 [107:1]).

In this Psalm and many others, we hear the command "give thanks to the Lord!" I tried to count how many times the Psalms mention giving thanks to God but I have to admit I gave up because there seemed to be so many! (Give it a try and let me know?!) When you hear the word thanksgiving you might think of Americans celebrating with a turkey, but the idea didn't originate with them. Not only is the idea of thanking God found in the Psalms, but all throughout the Bible. From thanksgiving sacrifices in the Old Testament to St Paul telling the readers of his letters to give thanks in the New Testament, and Jesus himself giving thanks to God the Father in the Gospels. **It is everywhere**. Despite this, giving thanks to God can occasionally be something that is brushed past, and the Bible verses that highlight this can go unnoticed. Seeing as it appears so many times it looks like it is actually a key part of getting to know God better and something He wants us to take notice of - so let's try!

Thank you for the fleas!

There is a true story that always reminds me that we should look for things to be thankful for even when things don't seem to be going well in our lives. There was a lady called Corrie Ten Boom who lived in the Netherlands during the Second World War. In her book 'The Hiding Place', Corrie shares how when the Jews were being taken away to concentration camps, her family who were Christian, hid them in their home. When the authorities found out, Corrie and her family were imprisoned in a concentration camp too. In the camp, the room that all the women had to sleep in was filled with thousands of fleas which just added to the discomfort of the place.

Yet in the midst of the horror of the camp and the conditions of their accommodation Corrie's sister Betsie insisted they must thank God for all things, including for the fleas, because God should be thanked in all circumstances and He could bring good from all things, even fleas. Understandably Corrie found this a bit difficult! But it turns out that because there were so many fleas the wardens never came into the room to avoid getting bitten, so Corrie and her sister were able to read from the Bible they'd smuggled in and spread the Gospel to everyone there. The fleas became a gift that brought them more freedom! They thanked God for the fleas when they didn't understand this - before they even knew that the fleas would be the very reason that other women in the camp were able to come to know the great gift of a relationship with Jesus and joy in the midst of great suffering. There is always more going on than we can see, so we shouldn't stop giving thanks because things look bad!

What does it mean to give thanks to God?

Saying thank you may seem like a simple idea, but what does it actually mean to give thanks to God? Being thankful for what we have is something that can be done by those who have no particular belief in God, but for Christians we focus our giving thanks towards God, the giver of these gifts, rather than sending out a general thanks into the atmosphere! **Giving thanks to God is actually a form of prayer**, so it is a fantastic way of developing your relationship with God and developing your prayer life. If you're ever not sure what to say to God in prayer, a great way to start is to thank Him for all that He has given you!

Giving thanks to God helps us to come to know Him more, because when we see more clearly that He has given us so many good things in our lives it teaches us how much He loves us. It shifts our focus from ourselves and our own problems to God and His unconditional love. People often exchange gifts to show they appreciate each other, and in the same way God gives us many gifts - though not always the material kind that are wrapped up in bright paper and tied with a bow! Every day if you wake up and you're still breathing, inhaling the morning air, you have a massive thing to be thankful for. God has given you the gift of today! The opportunity to live another day, to do the things we enjoy, to grow in the knowledge of His love through noticing the ways He blesses us, these are all God's gifts.

In James 1:17 it says that "Every generous act of giving, with every perfect gift, is from above, coming down from the Father of lights". All the good things that we experience in our lives can be seen as reflections of the great love that God has for us. God loves each one of us so much and giving thanks is choosing to take notice of this amazing truth. Even if we reach a point where we are finding it really hard to recognise anything to be thankful for, there will always be one thing, the ultimate gift that God gave us because of His love for us: **the forgiveness of our sins through the death and resurrection of Jesus Christ which means we can now have a relationship with Him and the hope of eternity with Him**. We can never give thanks enough for this greatest gift of all!

Give Me Joy In My Heart

If you ask anybody whether they want to be happy, you can be pretty sure they will tell you they do, but if you ask them how to achieve it they won't necessarily have an answer. Did you know that there have been scientific studies carried out that show that people who regularly list things they are thankful for become happier than those who don't? When we are grateful for what we have, this leads to joy. When we recognise all the good things in our lives that God has given us and done for us, it is hard not to smile. I remember singing a song when I was a child that had a line "a thankful heart is a happy heart" and it is true that when we begin to recognise all the amazing things around us, we can't help but be filled with joy and share it with others!

On his Twitter account Pope Francis said, "A Christian is never bored or sad. Rather, the one who loves Christ is full of joy and radiates joy." Joy is not the same as being happy all the time, but rather it comes from a deep knowledge of the goodness and love of God that is reflected in all the things He has done for us and given us. Sometimes this joy is expressed by singing, dancing and laughing, but at other times it is a quiet joy that enables us to keep going during the hard times when it would be easier to give up. Pope Francis talks about this in 'The Joy of the Gospel':

"There are Christians whose lives seem
like Lent without Easter. I realise of course

that joy is not expressed the same way at
all times of life, especially at moments of
great difficulty. Joy adapts and changes,
but it always endures, even as a flicker of
light born of our personal certainty that,
when everything is said and done, we are
infinitely loved."

A way to maintain this joy at all times of our lives is to keep finding things to be thankful for every single day. Thanksgiving is one of the keys to unlocking joy in our lives, but not just when things are going well. In fact, it is when things are hardest in life that having an attitude of gratitude can get us through. Colossians 3:17 says "whatever you do, in word or deed, do everything in the name of the Lord Jesus, giving thanks to God the Father through him". No matter whether we are out in the sunshine or tidying our bedroom, whether we are doing something easy or difficult, we should give thanks to God while we do it.

Just as Corrie ten Boom gave thanks for the fleas, sometimes we have to choose to give thanks for things even if they don't look good from our perspective. In St Paul's first letter to the Thessalonians he tells them to "give thanks in all circumstances" (1 Thessalonians 5:18). What, really? Every single circumstance? You might be thinking: "but you don't know all the bad the things I'm going through!" **The important thing to realise is that thanksgiving is not a way of pretending everything is fine or denying that a situation may be hard.** Life can be tough sometimes! But what thanksgiving does is it turns around the way we look at things; it helps us look for the good that is always present in the midst of the bad and the ways God's presence can still be seen in the difficult situations. We can learn to give thanks in every circumstance, even ones that people might ordinarily consider to be a negative, because we know that "all things work together for good for those who love God" (Romans 8:28). God can bring good out of the worst situation and so we can trust that God is still there loving us and give Him thanks for all the good that is still present in our lives.

"Giving thanks, He broke the bread…"

Jesus Himself gives us a model for thanksgiving in the Gospels. One of the times we see this is on the night before he was going to be put to death during the Last Supper when He had a meal with His followers. I think the likely reaction of someone who knew they were going to be killed the next day would be to be quite afraid and not really have giving thanks for things as their top priority. But in Luke 22:17-20, we see that during the meal Jesus still gave thanks:

> "Then he took a cup, and after giving thanks he said, 'Take this and divide it among yourselves, for I tell you that from now on I will not drink of the fruit of the vine until the kingdom of God comes.' Then he took a loaf of bread, and when he had given thanks, he broke it and gave it to them, saying 'This is my body, which is

Many people do the wonderful thing of saying grace before their meal to give thanks for the food, or they thank those who have made it. But what Jesus was doing was even deeper than this. Not only was He giving thanks for the food, He was giving thanks to God for His own death that was about to happen. As Catholics we believe that the bread and wine are transformed into the Body and Blood of Jesus (check out Chapter 8), so at the Last Supper, not only was Jesus giving thanks for the food, He was giving thanks for the breaking of His body that was about to happen – His sacrifice and death on the cross. In Hebrews 12:2 it says that for the "joy that was set before him [he] endured the cross, disregarding its shame, and has taken his seat at the right hand of the throne of God." Jesus recognised that God had a plan that was greater than pain and death and that it would lead to victory over sin – and for this He was filled with thanks and joy.

"It is right and just!"

For Catholics, the central part of our faith is the Mass. In the Mass we have the privilege of receiving Jesus fully present in the Eucharist, but do you know what this word actually means? The word Eucharist comes from the Greek word *eucharisteo* which means "to give thanks". So when we celebrate this each week, we are entering into a thanksgiving for Jesus giving up His life so that we could be forgiven and reconciled with God.

One of my favourite parts of the Mass is the preface to the Eucharistic prayer, which is the bit when we all proclaim "it is right and just!" On its own this proclamation doesn't make much sense, but what is it that we are saying is right and just? To give God thanks! The priest then goes on to say that "it is our duty and our salvation, always and everywhere, to give you thanks, Lord, Holy Father, Almighty and ever living God." Not only does this highlight St Paul's idea in his letters about giving thanks in every situation, but it is taken further by saying that giving thanks is our duty - something God expects us to do! Giving thanks is not meant to be an afterthought or something we do once in a while. **We are called to live lives of thanksgiving**.

How can I become more thankful?

So, we've established that giving thanks to God can transform our lives into lives of joy and help us become more aware of God's love, but how do we make this a reality in our lives and actually put thanksgiving into practise?

To travel along the journey of increasing in thankfulness, it's really important to first pray that God will help us. It is so easy to focus on the negative things, especially in a world where the media broadcasts news that is almost always bad and our default reaction is so often to complain. Ask God to open your eyes so that you can become even more aware of all the gifts He has placed in your life that you can be thankful for. We need to keep praying that God would enable us to live lives of thanksgiving, because it is through his Holy Spirit guiding us that we will be able to keep recognising His goodness in the things around us.

My own journey towards becoming more thankful began one New Year's Day when, armed with a little red notebook, I made a decision to begin writing down three things that I was thankful for every day. Inspired by a Canadian lady called Ann Voskamp who has written a lot about thanksgiving, I took up what she called a 'joy dare' to try to count one thousand things to be thankful to God for in the year ahead.

For me it has been life changing to write down three things I'm thankful for each day and has helped me to realise more how amazing the life that God gives us is. This has been a great way to get into a mind-set of being thankful and because I have to get into the habit of picking up a pen and writing I'm more likely to remember it; the notebook sits on my bedside table so it's difficult to forget about it!

There are different ways we can begin to give thanks more, and here are three practical things that can really help us:

> Why not pick up a pen and start counting all the great things about life? Writing down just three things every day that you are thankful for won't take more

than five minutes, but will make an amazing difference to the way you see life and God. Don't give up if you forget one day, just keep going!

➤ Another way of making thankfulness a bigger part of our lives is to have a time of giving thanks to God every day when praying. Perhaps before you go to sleep you could spend a few minutes thanking God for all the good things you experienced in the day.

➤ It is also great to remember to make the effort to thank others. We were all taught to say "please" and "thank you" when we were younger, but actually taking time to thank people for the things that they do for us can really impact them by showing we appreciate them and also help us to realise the way God blesses us through other people.

Don't give up giving thanks!

Growing in gratitude is a journey and it is often something that grows over time as our minds become more used to noticing all the good things around us. There are occasions when I find being thankful difficult and sometimes I have to remind myself to give thanks even when I really don't feel like it, but I have begun to learn that when you look hard enough, there are always so many things to be thankful for! Sometimes when I face challenging moments, I stop and remind myself of all the many things I have to be thankful for -

if I'm having a bad day it often turns my mood completely around to one of joy. Even if you're in a situation like sitting in a lesson at school wishing you were somewhere else, I challenge you to in that moment think of something, or more than one thing, to be thankful for as so many people across the world long to go to school!

Counting the ways God has blessed us fills us with His joy. **Sometimes the difference between a good day and a bad day is the way we look at it**; if we can see the ways God is present in it through all the blessings, it becomes a better day. Changing our perspective changes everything. We may not be able to change our circumstances, but we can change the way we look at them.

We can never run out of things to give thanks for, especially when we come to realise nothing is too small to be thankful for! People often talk about being thankful for the more obvious things like family and friends, or passing an exam. As incredible as these things are, there are numerous other blessings around us every day that we can sometimes miss if we don't stop to look for them. A life of thanksgiving means noticing the things easily missed, the seemingly small things we can thank God for, like my eyes to read these words, cool water that quenches my thirst, a smile from a friend or the amazing colours of summer flowers and autumn leaves. The list is endless! If we begin to recognise the gifts all around us, to count the many blessings, we can see how much God's love shines throughout our lives and all of creation.

What better way to document our lives than to list all of its blessings? When I look back over the pages full of thousands of things I have found to be thankful for, it paints a picture of the incredible love and mercy of God and His constant presence with us in the midst of the difficulties in our lives and our world. It demands a response of joy! Life is an incredible gift when it is seen through eyes that see God's presence in all places and recognise that, even in the tough moments, there is always, always something to be thankful for.

CHAPTER 3: WI-FI - PRAYER
Lewis Dowle

Connection Established

There are some key things to learn about prayer and this is gonna be a really cool chapter where you and I are going to be learning about what it means to pray. Prayer can often be thought of like Wi-Fi, a wireless connection. Only, this connection doesn't go slow or down in a storm. It's always there. We just need to make sure we are connected. The network name for the router is "God_Loves_You" and the password is "Jesus_Saves". Plug this in an you're good to go.

Prayer is a conversation. I probably don't need to write about what a conversation is, I imagine you've all been in at least one! Now it is important to note here that the word is *conversation*; what this means is that there are at least two people involved in some form of dialogue. In the case of prayer, it means we talk to God, **and God talks to us.** Maybe you're thinking, God speaks to me!? And I know it sounds crazy, but it's true. And the coolest part is the fact that **He wants to speak to us.** Prayer doesn't need to be always on our knees, it doesn't have to be in a church and we can speak to God directly.

Like Wi-Fi, as long as we are in the router's range we can connect to the internet, only that with God's router it expands across the whole universe! There is **nowhere** in our galaxy you could travel to which would say, "No connection" if you tried to pray. With God it's also like going on Skype. We can scroll down through our contacts and we so often just see "Busy" or "Do not disturb" from our friends; many people in our lives may not want to hear from us for various reasons. **But God does.** On Skype, beside God's name it will always say "Available". And like instant messenger, we can speak to God differently, with text, audio and video.

You know that feeling when you're absolutely exhausted and just wanna chill with some friends and you don't even have to say anything? Well prayer can be like that as well. And in the same way we can communicate with each other in **words** (like in English or Elvish), **writing** and **actions**, so too can we communicate with God in different ways. Prayer can be in the form of the Mass and the Rosary (check out Chapters 4 and 6), but it can also be when we're doing homework, or playing the violin or singing to God, or kneeling in your room, or reading your Bible on the beach, or visiting your grandmother. **Our whole lives can be our prayer.**

One, two, three, four. One, two, three, four...

Maybe you've played in an orchestra before or you may be in a band with some friends. If you have, the word **rhythm** is very important. How does rhythm work? **We need to listen.** To stay in beat with the band you need to make sure you're counting the same beats in a bar. Can you imagine if a whole orchestra played with sound-muting ear plugs? Do you think they'll be in perfect harmony? Chances are they'll get lost. And quickly. You see, God is like the conductor and the composer, but he's also playing the songs with us. And to make the song sound good we need to be following the conductor. Prayer is that listening.

Or perhaps you're into football. The best players are often said to have good 'vision'. What they mean by this is that they're looking up, searching for the best passes and look to see where their team and the opposition are. To always have your head looking at your feet in football will mean you won't know when to pass or when you're going to receive the ball. Prayer is looking up, looking at where we can receive the ball when we don't have it, and when we can pass it if we do.

Why do we pray?

It's important to say that **prayer doesn't change God: it changes us.** The YouCat (470) says this: "Praying is as human as breathing, eating, and loving. Praying purifies. Praying makes it possible to resist temptations. Praying strengthens us in our weakness. Praying removes fear, increases energy, and gives a second wind. Praying makes one happy." Those seem good enough reasons to me!

You may have been told by an adult, "Don't hang around with him, he's a rough 'un" or maybe, "She isn't a good influence on you, you'll end up like her if you're not careful." Who we spend time with is **incredibly** important. And who better is there to spend time with than the very One who made time! The more time we spend with Jesus, the more we will be like Him, the more full of peace we'll be, the more excited about our faith we'll be. We also find in the YouCat (469) that "When a person prays, he enters into a living relationship with God." To be in a relationship with God is to be in a friendship which none compares to. So often we can be at church and 'living relationship' would not be the words we would often use to describe our parishes! But God invites us into a relationship **which is alive.**

How to pray?

So **how** do we pray? Just as there are many ways to get to London, so there are many ways to pray. I could ride a bike, I could take a car, I could fly, I could ride a penguin, I could drive a tank, I could go by submarine or even hop backwards whilst wearing an angry birds hat (it's possible). We can come to God in many different ways which we will come back to, but as in all aspects of our faith, turning to the Bible is always a great place to start. This very question of how to pray was asked to Jesus 2,000 years ago and it is the same response for us today.

"He was praying in a certain place, and
after he had finished, one of his disciples
said to him, 'Lord, teach us to pray, as
John taught his disciples.' He said to them,
'When you pray, say:
Father, hallowed be your name.

Your kingdom come.
Give us each day daily bread.
And forgive us our sins,
for we ourselves forgive everyone indebted
to us.
And do not bring us to the time of trial.'"
(Luke 11:1-4).

This is one of the two occasions Jesus talks about what we would know today as the 'Our Father' prayer or the 'Lord's prayer' (check out Matthew 6:9-13).

The YouCat teaches us that we can't learn to pray in the same way that we could learn other things. If you were to learn the guitar, your teacher will tell you the correct technique, how that if you practice the same scales everyday you'll soon be breaking out into guitar solos. Or with sewing. Googling how to make different patterns will allow you to soon make them, following careful instructions, following them word-for-word. But prayer isn't quite the same. The YouCat (469) says this, "As strange as it sounds, prayer is a gift one obtains through prayer." **We learn to pray by praying!** It's an exercise of faith where we put our trust in God for Him to lead the way. We could read lots on prayer, but the best way to grow in it is to simply give prayer a go!

Sssshhhh!

Jesus in the Bible also tells us in Matthew 6:6 that "whenever you pray, go into your room and shut the door and pray to your Father". Find somewhere you feel comfortable to pray in; maybe its your room, maybe its your garden or local church, but feeling comfortable is key. "Shut your door" are Jesus' words and this can be a physical closing of a door so we can enter into quiet, or it can be shutting the door to Twitter or Facebook for five minutes, or leaving our phones in the house as we pray outside. Saint Mother Theresa said that "In the silence of the heart God speaks. If you face God in prayer and silence, God will speak to you." For hundreds of years loads of Saints have discovered the power of prayer and of silence. Everything around us is so noisy, so relentlessly distracting, to put everything on silent for just a few minutes a day can allow God to put things back in order in our lives.

So silence is a great way to pray, **just sitting and listening.** God is always speaking to us in so many ways, not just in a voice we can hear. It can be a sense such as God prompting you to text your friend who has just broken their arm, or to make an effort with that person you struggle with at school. God could speak to you through song lyrics. Maybe in the silence a song comes into your mind which God may be speaking to you through. You might in the silence see a picture in your head of something. We can ask God what it means. The thing is, God is speaking to us in loads of cool ways and **every time we pray it can be different.**

Feeling in the Desert

Don't worry if you feel 'dry' when you pray. Often we can feel as if no one is there when we are praying and that it isn't worth our prayer time. Remember on Facebook

Messenger God is always online, even if we appear offline. The Bible says in 1 John 5:14 that "this is the boldness we have in him, that if we ask anything according to his will, **he hears us**" (emphasis added). There is a great tip in our relationship with God which I heard from a friend: **We walk by faith and not by feelings.** When we pray, we may not *feel* like God is listening, in fact we often don't *feel* anything at all. **And that is ok.**

So much of the world around us is about how things make us feel and God simply wants us to trust Him. In our prayer we may feel His presence, but don't worry if you don't. Some Saints didn't feel God's presence for years and years (check out Chapter 11); but here's the trick: **to pray anyway.** Mark Hart of LifeTeen said on Twitter "Pray...especially when you don't feel like it" (8th July, 2014).

Merci, Danke, Grazie

Silence is a great way to pray, but another easy way to start is **to say thank you.** Now, there may be many times where saying thank you is not at all what you are feeling, especially after a long day of school, but let's expand on this.

In Scripture, it says: "**give thanks in all circumstances**; for this is the will of God in Christ Jesus for you" (1 Thessalonians 5:18, emphasis added). Looking at this again we see it says in **all** circumstances. So how does this work out for you and I? **There is always something to be grateful for** (check out Chapter 2 again). Although you weren't top of the class in science, you still have the privilege to be at school; and maybe you have a bad cold, but you can still see and hear perfectly. So much of life is our perspective and keeping a focus on God can make us see things differently.

Days can often be frantic but a good way to pray is at the end of the day looking back over the things you have done. They may be thanking God for the sunshine, or for the music exam going well, or the dance recital being the best yet, or that your aunt is feeling better, or that you did well in a test at school. Things can be difficult around us, but saying thank you to God and focusing on the good things around us can make the trickier situations seem less scary.

Fibre Optic Connection

I was abroad a few years ago. As I arrived to stay with some family friends, there was news of a teenaged boy, James, from their youth group who was having an operation the following day. It turned out it was an operation on a brain tumour. God worked so powerfully in this difficult situation and He brought His full healing to James! What had happened was this.

James was playing sport when he suffered concussion during a school match. To check up that he was ok after the concussion, the medics decided to do a scan. The scan went up to the very bottom of James' head. The doctors noticed something that was out of the ordinary and so decided to do a full scan on his brain. James had a brain tumour the size of a peach. They had to operate as soon as they could, unsure of what could be done for the boy. This is where prayer comes into its own. James' school, the youth group, his family, his friends, they all prayed. I messaged people around the world to pray. We were united in this wireless connection with God.

The operation was meant to take a couple of hours, but took more, and then some more. After being in the operating theatre for almost nine hours James came around. A couple of weeks later I could meet James for the first time, who you would never have been able to tell he had had a brain tumour at all! God had completely healed him. **We can pray to God, and God hears us.**

Keep Calm and Pray

Many of us, and myself included, often separate our lives into categories. Simply: prayer and not-prayer time. It says in the Bible however:

"pray without ceasing"
(1 Thessalonians 5:17).

But how are we to pray at all times when we might be studying, or acting, or working, or chilling? This is something we work on our whole lives. **The life we live can all be a**

prayer, it can all be a form of worship to God. So this means that we can speak to God **continually.** We can speak to God before the maths test or before the basketball match. We can tell God we're finding physics difficult (again) and ask him for help. **God delights in hearing us.** One of the most important parts of prayer is that **God is more excited for you to pray than you are.** Sometimes it is very easy to pray, when we feel on top of the world and that everything is going really well. But in times where we're struggling and lack any motivation for prayer, know that God is waiting and looking for you to come back into His arms.

There was once a father who had two sons. The younger of the two sons decided he wanted to live it up in a foreign land and asked for his inheritance early, pretty much saying to the father "I can't be bothered to wait for you to die, I want my money now". The father was hurt by the son but decided to accept his son's decision and split the inheritance between the son and his brother. After spending all the money on wild parties, the son soon found himself with no money or friends. He decided to find a job feeding pigs, but he soon realised that the pigs had more to eat than he did.

The son decided enough was enough and that he would return back to his father apologising for all that he had done. He was making his way home when his father, who was looking out, saw his son. This was the son who had crushed his father's heart. Do you know what the father did? He ran to him. He hugged him, he embraced him and he kissed him. The son tried to say sorry for all he had done wrong but the father was too bubbling with joy to respond, instead he called for the finest clothes, the finest food and a ring to be placed on his son. The father rejoiced because his son who was lost was found, his son who was dead was now alive.

That story as you may know is from the Bible (check out Luke 15:11-32). The people in the story are real, even though Jesus was telling it as a parable (a story which reveals something about who God is). The son represents you and I, and the father is God. **When we come back to God, no matter where we have been, God runs to us to embrace us and welcome us in as His dear children.**

May this be an encouragement to us all in our prayer life. Perhaps you haven't prayed in a long time; it may be that you have never prayed. Remember, when we come to God, He runs to us and is desperate to tell us how much He loves you and I. And well, thinking about that seems to make prayer seem a whole lot easier...

But to make things even easier, let's look at some practical tips to help us pray.

10 Tips for Prayer

1. **God hears you even if you don't 'hear' Him.** In prayer, we can speak to God about anything and everything and He always listens to us (even if you have told Him for the fiftieth time today you want to marry Taylor Swift). He loves to hear your voice and will always welcome you into His arms. If we don't seem to 'hear' Him, know that God speaks to us in

many ways. Trusting that He listens to our words is a great way to start thinking about prayer, but also know that He speaks and is moving in our lives when we pray even when we don't feel anything.

2.   **Don't worry if your mind wanders again and again**.   To keep our minds entirely focused in prayer isn't easy. We can so easily start to pray and then think all about the upcoming football matches (at least I do...), but each time we refocus our minds for prayer is prayer in itself. "The desire to pray is already a prayer" (Georges Bernanos). God sees our hearts and delights that we set aside time to pray - even if our mind wanders for most of it!

3.   **Mix up your prayer life!** There are loads of different types of prayer and don't worry about trying out different types of prayer and mixing it up. One day you may feel like just sitting in quiet for a couple of minutes, the next you may feel like listening to your favourite Christian song and singing along to the words of it. Or maybe the next day you go to daily Mass and the day after try to learn a worship song on the piano. Or perhaps the day after that you feel like writing a prayer journal of all the things on your heart and then decide the day after to go for a prayer walk or run. Or maybe even after that you feel like meeting up with a friend to learn to pray the Rosary and then decide the day after to read you Bible. You could also decide to try and learn to pray the Church's Divine Office joining the worldwide 24/7 prayer of the

Church prayed by priests, monks, sisters, teens and many others. And maybe the day after that read a Christian book or poem. There are so many types of prayer and it's great to try them all and to keep your prayer life fresh. Mix it up.

4.   **Know that God cares for you**. When we enter into prayer, God wants to take away all anxiety, all our tiredness and struggles and to fill us with life, joy, peace and blessings. Jesus said, "Come to me, all you that are weary and are carrying heavy burdens, and I will give you rest" (Matthew 11:28). God wants to refresh and revive us (check out Psalm 22 [23]). St Peter also tells us, "Cast all your anxiety on him, because he cares for you" (1 Peter 5:7). No matter how we are feeling, we can come to God and give Him all that is weighing us down and He will lift us up in joy and peace.

5.   **Don't worry if you don't 'feel' anything**. Although we often don't 'feel' anything in prayer, it doesn't mean that our prayer was a waste of time. God sees us and hears us when we pray. Always. Feelings come and go like the wind and it is dangerous to build our life only on feelings. Feelings can be great as they could help lead us more fervently into prayer, but it often happens that feelings can weigh us down and discourage us from entering into prayer. In my own life I quite often don't 'feel' anything when I pray. But even more often are the many times I choose not to pray and then feel in my whole being an invitation

into prayer again.

6. **Be relaxed when you pray**. We can pray anywhere and being comfortable is very important. Kneeling when we pray is a great position to pray and it works for some people as it reminds them to keep their focus on God, but it isn't any 'better' than lying on your bed, or sitting on a beanbag. If you find you focus and pray better whilst sitting on an inflatable shark, go for it. Any position or place which leads you to think about God and pray better is great. Again, feel free to mix it up, you may sit in your room one day and then visit your local church the day after.

7. **We can ask God to help us pray**. Just as the disciples asked Jesus to teach them to pray, so too can we ask God for help. God is so delighted to hear His children's voices, He will be wanting us to learn to pray even more than we do. We can often become fixed in habits and routines in prayer where we don't think about what we're praying but just rattling off a list. Asking God to teach us to pray can help us with this. Try not to get weighed down with prayer. We can often get into mindsets where "Unless I pray the Rosary 9 times a day God won't love me". God loves us unconditionally, whether we pray or whether we don't, and it sounds strange, but it is because of this that we should want to pray! In Scripture, it says that "where the Spirit of the Lord is, there is freedom" (2 Corinthians 3:17) which means that we are free in prayer. Don't worry if you struggle in this area, many

of us do, but during our whole lives we will grow more in prayer and God will lead us. We can ask Him and He will show us the way to go!

8.   **Open your heart to God**. Now by this I don't mean open heart surgery. When we pray, we can enter into prayer with an open or closed heart. Many go to church and pray, but with no openness to God and no desire to change. God loves us so much He doesn't want to leave us the way we are. He wants to make us like Him and we need to be open and willing to change. Being open to God opens the doors for every blessing, every joy and opportunities which would blow our minds.

9.   **Start small**. If you've never really prayed before, don't worry. Starting can seem daunting but starting small is best. Try for praying just a couple of minutes maybe in the morning. It's a great way to start the day. Soon after you might decide to just sit in quiet after a long day at school. The next month you may feel like trying to read your Bible on the bus. Don't start with praying for seven hours straight! Prayer is like exercise where we work up to a marathon. If we tried to run for 26 miles without ever practicing, we would be put off running for life! So too with prayer, starting small is always best.

10.   **Keep going!** Try not to get disheartened if you find prayer hard. Again, starting out small is best and then just keep going! If you find that you forget to

pray for a few days, don't worry. Just try again! And
after that if you forget to pray, don't get cross at
yourself, just try again! Prayer will soon become
second nature. God is excited to hear your voice again,
even if it's been a long time.

CHAPTER 4: ARMY TRAINING – THE ROSARY
Serena Wong

Serena is a missionary from Malaysia, born in a beautiful town called Kota Kinabalu. She is passionate about affirming and restoring human dignities, loves flowers and the colour blue.

"Give me an army saying the Rosary and I will conquer the world." Pope Blessed Pius IX

We all know that God, in the beginning as He created the world, created man on the sixth day, and He "created humankind in his image, in the image of God he created them; male and female he created them"(Genesis 1:27). We all have been taught about the fall of mankind for not obeying God's command. Adam and Eve were sent out of the Garden of Eve. We all have fallen short of God's glory (Romans 3:23).

Then, there came the story of salvation talked about earlier in this book (Chapter 1), where God, in His mercy and greatness, sent His only Son Jesus Christ to restore the glory and dignity of mankind. "For the love of Christ urges us on, because we are convinced that one has died for all; therefore all have died. And he died for all, so that those who live might live no longer for themselves, but for him who died and was raised for them" (2 Corinthians 5:14-15).

Have we ever asked ourselves, why would someone die

for us? And how is it that this man's death would lead to life for all? These are significant questions to reflect upon on our journey of faith, because it gives us strength and understanding of who we are, and also whom God is.

To answer these questions, the twenty beautiful mysteries that are presented in the Rosary give a very profound understanding of the reasons Jesus led His life the way He did. He did it for you and I to grow fuller and deeper each day and to become the Saint we are called to be.

Let us take time to reflect, through the intercession of our Beloved Mother Mary, upon these beautiful mysteries. And if you've never prayed the Rosary before, flick to the end of the chapter[1]!

The Joyful Mysteries (Monday and Saturday)

First Joyful Mystery - The Annunciation of the Archangel to Mary

God is Adventurer! I am adventurous!

Everyone desires adventures. That's why we love super heroes and heroines – Spiderman, the Hulk, Superman,

---

[1] Please note that the use of words "man" and "men" refers to all humanity, both men and women, unless specified otherwise.

Wolverine, Rapunzel, Cat Woman, Elsa and Anna from Frozen, you name it. **Deep down in each of us, we want to live life in an adventure, to do great things.**

In this mystery, Mary, as a young teen responded boldly to be the mother of Christ. Knowing the risks that she may go through, she still responded with, "let it be with me according to your word" (Luke 1:38). By her heroic "Yes" to God, it led to Jesus bringing salvation to the world.

God created man – Adam, and entrusted the Garden of Eden to him, "The LORD God took the man and put him in the garden of Eden to till it and keep it" (Genesis 2:15). The man was to name all the animals and plants. Therefore, it is by this nature that man was instilled with the desire to inquire and explore.

The desire for adventure could also been seen in the new Adam, our Lord Jesus. The Salvation was planned by the Father, the Son and the Spirit. The Son took on this adventure knowing clearly what was asked of Him and what He would go through. Jesus said, "I lay it down of my own accord" (John 10:18). Jesus was anxious too. But He knew what was ahead and made the choice to pay the price despite it, for the greater victory.

As each adventure of our lives is presented to us, may we respond courageously with a "Yes" to conquer and gain victory. **You are called to be heroic!**

Second Joyful Mystery – Mary's Visitation to Elizabeth

God is the Truth! I am true!

We desire to be our true self. Everyone is unique. Just like the super heroes that we admire, they are all unique with their own super powers. We, too, possess this uniqueness. Do you know that no one's finger prints and DNA are the same? This is how **one-of-a-kind we are**. God is the greatest Sculptor and Creator. He is never out of ideas and loves originality in all that He creates. So, how do we find our true selves?

To find our true selves, Jesus is the key to the discovery. He brings about true freedom and pure joy. In this mystery, John leapt in his mother's womb when Mother Mary greeted Elizabeth. Similarly, we will be filled with the same joy when we come to meet Jesus in person because our true identity will be revealed.

Many of us may be fearful to find this true identity. However, here is the reality. Jesus, even in His most vulnerable state on the cross, having left his glorious Throne and taken off His Majestic Robe, still reflected His dignity. This is because He knew most certainly who He was. He never forgot the very first message He received when He was baptised by John the Baptist, Heaven opened and there came a Voice saying, "You are my Son, the Beloved; with you I am well pleased" (Mark 1:11).

On the day you were baptised, Heaven opened and God declared that you are His Beloved too and He very much delights in you.

Allow yourself time to spend with Jesus and ask Him to reveal more of who you are in God's eyes.

Third Joyful Mystery – The Birth of Jesus, the Messiah

God nurtures. I am nurtured.

We desire to be nurtured. We want to receive the undivided attention that will bring about encouragement and support along our journey. This is especially true when we first entered into the world.

We all love Christmas. Beyond the gifts and feasts that fill this special occasion, it is the Day we celebrate the birth of our Lord Jesus. When Jesus entered into the world, He was born of the Virgin Mary, who was accompanied and protected by a foster father, Saint Joseph. Jesus, too, was given a mother and a father to love and nurture Him as He grew and went on His mission.

In Psalm 120:7 [121:7], God promises that He will guard you from all harm and that He guards your life. He will never forsake you. He initiates and is truthful to this Promise to nurture you.

Fourth Joyful Mystery – The Presentation in the Temple

God is Holy. I am holy.

Deep down in each of us, we have the great desire to be holy. "You shall be holy to me; for I the LORD am holy, and I have separated you from other peoples to be mine" (Leviticus 20:26).

It is God's desire to have all men consecrated to Him. It is out of His generous love that He wants to consecrate us and set us apart as His own. This is intended to lead us to see things beyond and above every situation we may be in. This journey brings about the process of sanctification and purification in us to become who we are meant to be.

Jesus was also set apart for a great mission since the day He was born. Forty days after Jesus' birth, Mary and Joseph brought Him to the temple to be circumcised and consecrated to the Lord as the Law of the Lord was written (Luke 2:21-23). At this, Simeon prophesied to Mary, "This child is destined for the falling and the rising of many in Israel, and to be a sign that will be opposed" (Luke 2:34).

Like every one of us, Jesus was on a journey discovering His mission on earth. But this consecration was crucial for the discovery of His calling. St John wrote this, "Beloved, we are God's children now; what we will be has not yet been revealed. What we do know is this: when he is revealed, we will be like him, for we will see him as he is. And all who have this hope in him purify themselves, just as he is pure" (1 John 3:2-3).

Let's make the decision today to consecrate ourselves to the Lord in order that God's great purpose in us will be fulfilled. **We are called to be holy, made worthy by God to build and inherit the Kingdom of God.**

Fifth Joyful Mystery – Finding the Boy Jesus in the Temple

God is Wisdom. I am wise.

We are all thirsting and seeking for wisdom. We are curious about the world – animals, plants, the galaxy, biology, physics, chemistry, a list that could be unending and people from all generations have tried to seek an understanding of it. It was Wisdom who protected the first man to be fashioned (Wisdom 10:1).

As a result, many strive to study within a formal education structure, from kindergarten through to university or on their personal initiative to learn more in various ways. We are to be cautious where we are to seek our wisdom and knowledge from.

The beginning of wisdom is the fear (awe) of God (Proverbs 9:10). This mystery speaks of Jesus growing in age and wisdom, sought always from the Source. He, at the age of twelve, was found in the Temple, a place of God's presence and a Source to grow. He sat among the teachers, listened to them, and asked questions (Luke 2:45-46). All those who heard Him, including the Pharisees and Scribes, were astounded at His intelligence and His replies (Luke 2:47).

The depth and width of wisdom one could go into is unlimited. Therefore, the more we study, the more we know what we do not know. In addition, many of us can misuse the little that we thought we understood about something. We have learned to analyse and assume.

It is important for us to always tap into wisdom, God's Wisdom, and use what we have learnt to good use and to stand for the Truth.

The Luminous Mysteries (Thursday)

First Luminous Mystery – The Baptism of the Lord

God is the Loving Father. I am His beloved child.

We want to belong to a group as a reflection of who we are as an individual but on a larger scale. This speaks of our identity. We join orchestras, clubs, ministries, teams and so on and we fight to raise the dignity and victory of that identity, where we belong.

Adam was created out of love by God and for God. He

belonged to God. But because of the Fall, the relationship was dented. He was sent out of the Garden of eternal happiness. However, God's abounding love and mercy led Him to a decision of bringing salvation to all humanity. Jesus was sent by God for you and I. What's more, with Jesus' presence as a man, we received the gift of Baptism.

When Jesus was baptised by John, there was a voice from heaven, "This is my Son, the Beloved, with whom I am well pleased" (Matthew 3:17). **Through Baptism, we receive the restoration of the Father-Son relationship with our Heavenly Father.** He called us "the Beloved" and we return to the place where we have always belonged.

Second Luminous Mystery – The Wedding at Cana in Galilee

God is ever New. I am transformed.

New things, new people, new environments and new experiences always attract people. Life seems to be stagnant and boring if there seems to be nothing new. We praise and thank God not only because of His steadfast love that never ceases, but also because His mercies never come to an end and He fills us with them anew every morning (Lamentations 3:22-23)! He is the portion of our souls and brings transformation in our lives (Lamentations 3:24).

This gift of newness and transformation is readily

available. It requires our response to be open to receive it.

Performing a miracle at the Wedding at Cana, Jesus asked the servants to fill the jars with water to the brim and then to draw some out for the master of the feast to taste. At that instant of tasting, the water had been transformed into good wine (John 2:6-10).

We are invited to empty ourselves like the empty jars. With that, we are invited to be open to allow God to fill us with every good gift and work of Him. Each of these gifts are meant to cleanse and purify us as the water is. When we come openly into the presence of God all the days of our lives, we are transformed, and people whom we meet and talk to will experience and taste the goodness and sweetness of who we are and the Source of this. We become a new person each day. This is the only newness that will fulfil our thirst and hunger for new experiences.

Third Luminous Mystery – Jesus Proclaims the Kingdom of God

God is the General. I am a warrior.

We are warriors of the Kingdom of Heaven. We desire to conquer. Why are we called warriors? All warriors through the ages fight for the protection of their earthly kingdoms and fellow countrymen. In this conquest, we, as the warriors of God's Kingdom, are also called to protect and build with zeal our Heavenly Kingdom through the salvation of souls. This desire to conquer comes from the vision to build this Kingdom with Faith, Hope and Love.

When Jesus began His ministry, He said to the crowd, "The time is fulfilled, and the kingdom of God has come near; repent, and believe in the good news" (Mark 1:15). From that moment, He began to call His disciples. The call to evangelise for this Kingdom falls honourably on each of us who belong to it. This is the great commissioning for all of us to go out to the whole world, to proclaim the Gospel to all creation (Mark 16:15).

As you strive to conquer, stand on your ground, with Truth a belt round your waist, and Righteousness a breastplate, wearing shoes on your feet the eagerness to spread the Gospel of Peace, and always carrying the shield of Faith so that you can use it to quench the burning arrows of the Evil One. And you must take Salvation as your helmet and the sword of the Spirit: the Word of God (Ephesians 6:14-17).

Remember that we have a General, Jesus Christ, who goes before us and fights for us.

Fourth Luminous Mystery – The Transfiguration

God is Light. I shine.

We desire to shine. We are all called for a great purpose.

St Irenaeus said, "The Glory of God is man fully alive." **We shine when we are living out our passions, which are God-planted ones in the depths of our hearts.** These passions are meant to build on the Kingdom of God.

While Jesus was praying His face changed in appearance and His clothing became dazzling white. And behold two men were talking with Him, Moses and Elijah, who appeared in glory and spoke of His exodus that He was going to accomplish in Jerusalem (Luke 9:28-31). This event also shows us a glimpse of who we will be, as part of the glorious Church, united with God, the Saints and the angelic host.

We are the reflection of God's glory. This is flowing from the Source of our Creator – the Lord. As the One sitting on the throne, like a diamond and a ruby, encircled by a rainbow, like an emerald, God is charming and He draws people to Himself (Revelations 4:3). So do men reflect the glory of God (1 Corinthians 11:7).

However, this Kingdom, or what we call Heaven, does not only appear above the clouds or in the life to come, it is now, wherever and whenever the presence of God is recognised and lived. We all like good sensations and many of us might say, "Oh, it's heaven" when we feel comfortable, eat delicious food or being in the company of good friends. These things can be a foretaste of things yet to come!

We desire a place of joy and peace now. Hence, God desires us to shine and bring forth this glorious side of ourselves as we live our calling and give our best.

Fifth Luminous Mystery – The Institution of the Eucharist

God is Communion. I am consumed.

We desire intimacy. We want to be held, adored and loved.

As Jesus gave Himself in the Eucharist, He desires intimacy with us. "Those who eat my flesh and drink my blood abide in me, and I in them" (John 6:56). In the depths of our hearts we all long for this intimacy and many desire to take vows for life-long commitment in order to deepen this intimacy.

This desire for intimacy is strongly illustrated in this verse:

"As the Father has loved me, so I have loved you; abide in my love. If you keep my commandments, you will abide in my love, just as I have kept my Father's commandments and abide in his love. I have said these things to you so that my joy may be in you, and that your joy may be complete."
(John 15:9-11).

He desires an intimate union with you and I, one that brings everlasting joy.

The Sorrowful Mysteries (Tuesday and Friday)

First Sorrowful Mystery – Jesus prays at the Garden of Gethsemane

God transcends. I am free.

We need space. We want to have our own rooms and freedom to express ourselves.

When man was first created, he lived in perfect harmony with God and God alone. As a man lives his daily life, the interaction with others uses up his energy and power. It is essential for man to spend time in solitude, to recharge our batteries.

Jesus embraced times of retreat in the midst of His mission work. "And after he had dismissed the crowds, he went up the mountain by himself to pray. When evening came, he was there alone" (Matthew 14:23). Especially in times of anguish and heavy burdens, a time to be alone is very important. Jesus did this before His Passion. He prayed in the garden of Gethsemane in complete solitude seeking His Father's strength (Mark 14:32-39).

Jesus felt the need to be on His own to regain His power, to ponder on His higher destiny, His human nature and His entire dependence on the Father. He could not do His work or maintain His fellowship in power without His space and quiet time. His isolation (or need for space) is not a gesture of Him withdrawing His love. Rather, He loves so deeply that He chooses solitude so that He can give more of Himself - His very best. Sometimes we need to do the same. To spend time alone means we can give more for the glory of God.

Second Sorrowful Mystery – The Scourging at the Pillar

God is Protector. I am protected.

All of us desire to be protected. However, my personal reflection on this mystery is that men are called to be the protectors as Jesus was, while women are the protected.

Woman was created by taking a rib out of Adam's side, close to the heart of the man. Like a knight in shining armour, a man desires to protect a woman as the knight protects and defends his kingdom. This is because "This at last is bone of my bones and flesh of my flesh; this one shall be called Woman, for out of man this one was taken" (Genesis 2:23).

Like Jesus who took on the scourging at the pillar to bear all our sins so that we would live in righteousness and holiness (1 Peter 2:24), a man is created to desire, to protect and defend woman so her holiness and beauty remain sacred.

Third Sorrowful Mystery – The Crowning of Thorns

God is Beauty. I am beautiful.

As Jesus who took on the crown of thorns because He could not stand seeing His beloved ones tarnished by the stain and ugliness of sin (Matthew 27:29), so do men desire true beauty. We desire beauty because we are reminded of the Source of Beauty and Perfection. Both men and women are created to be beautiful but those who strive towards holiness will exude true and lasting beauty, which real men desire, embrace and treasure (Proverbs 31:30).

The holiness and virtues that Mother Mary holds are true beauty that every man would desire. God is the Creator and Beholder of Beauty. As such, He crowned Mother Mary as Queen of Heaven (Revelations 12:1). Blessed are the men who embrace beauty as they come to see the Creator and Beholder of   Beauty.

Fourth Sorrowful Mystery – The Carrying of the Cross

God is Strength. I am strong.

All men desire to be strong, to be the pillars for their loved ones.

The message that society sends out today is that those who are strong are capable and the victors. The word "strong" has been distorted to include only physical strength. For example at school, we see bullies and we would term them as the stronger ones. Those who excel in sports are the popular kids around the block. But how does Jesus show us the real meaning of strength?

Jesus carried His cross, the weight of all our sins, on the road to Calvary (John 19:17). On this journey, though spat at, mocked and tortured, Jesus remained silent and persevered until the end. The one true and only factor that carried Him to the end is His love for you and I. And this is what it is: **Love brings strength and Love *is* Strength.**

Therefore, we are invited to tap into the Source of Strength, who will give us the same strength and power that raised Jesus Christ from the dead and enthroned Him at the Father's right hand in heaven (Ephesians 1:20).

Here, I would like to add in a particular note to the ladies. The world today teaches us to the fight for equality in all aspects of our lives. Be affirmed that God makes no mistakes in creating us in our gentleness and vulnerability. Jesus made Himself vulnerable at His birth through to His crucifixion to bring us the greatest gift of Life. We need to embrace our identity and nature as women. These are the qualities that are essentially required to bring God's presence to the world.

Real strength requires wisdom and in many situations, what seems weak and gentle, is actually the reflection of real strength. Here I would like to share this

Scripture from St Paul as our reflection:

"but he said to me, "My grace is sufficient
for you, for power is made perfect in
weakness." So, I will boast all the more
gladly of my weaknesses, so that the power
of Christ may dwell in me. Therefore I am
content with weaknesses, insults,
hardships, persecutions, and calamities for
the sake of Christ; for whenever I am
weak, then I am strong."
(2 Corinthians 12:9-11).

Fifth Sorrowful Mystery – Jesus is Crucified

God is Love. I am loved.

We are called to love as Christ loved. True love brings forth vulnerability because when we love, we pour out our hearts and give our lives, not even knowing if this love will be reciprocated. **True love gives even before it receives.** Jesus placed Himself in a vulnerable state, to love and save us even if that love is never shared.

Greater love has no one than this, than to lay down one's life for his friends (John 15:13). True love can be seen through the coming of Jesus Christ and His Crucifixion. He came as the Lamb for sacrifice (Revelations 5:6), taking off His Majestic

Robe and climbing down from His Throne for the salvation of all humankind. He chose to die for you and I, "For our sake he made him to be sin who knew no sin, so that in him we might become the righteousness of God" (2 Corinthians 5:21). God "proves his love for us in that while we were still sinners Christ died for us" (Catechism of the Catholic Church [CCC], 604; Romans 5:8).

Therefore, every time we feel discouraged, lonely, distressed or anguished, take time to look at the Crucifix. Remember that we have the love and salvation of "Jesus of Nazareth, the King of the Jews" (John 19:19). As Saint Josemaria Escriva said, Jesus "is the Christ on the cross, a God who suffers and dies, a God who gives us His heart opened by a lance for the love of us all." The Crucifix is a symbol of vulnerability and love in great victory and dignity. It is a gift of Love, the 'passport' that is freely given to us who choose to receive Jesus and the eternal life He offers us. As St. Rose of Lima said, "Apart from the cross there is no other ladder by which we may get to heaven."

The Glorious Mysteries (Wednesday and Sunday)

First Glorious Mystery – The Resurrection of Jesus

God is Life. I am alive.

When God entrusted the Garden of Eden to the care of Adam, He invited and called men to receive life and also to be co-creators of life. All through the ages, we can clearly see God's Heart for eternal life through the many second chances that He gave generously to Abraham, Noah, King David, Peter, Paul, and gives to you and I.

"For God so loved the world that he gave his only Son, so that everyone who believes in him may not perish but have eternal life. Indeed, God did not send the Son into the world to condemn the world, but in order that the world might be saved through him" (John 3:16-17).

This is Jesus' Mission to the world, "I came that they may have life, and have it abundantly" (John 10:10).

Like receiving any gifts during Christmas or on our birthdays, we receive them with joy and a great appreciation. Most importantly, the gifts are used for their purposes.

Therefore, when we receive life from Jesus, we are called to live it out for the great purposes for which we are

created. When we respond as such, we become fully alive and bring about change to the world.

Second Glorious Mystery – The Ascension of Jesus

God is the Provider. I have enough.

Men, through the ages, strive towards fulfilment within their lives. We want to have enough, and even more than enough, to be the providers for our loved ones in terms of shelter, food, clothing, security, and all that is needed.

Jesus in the pursuit of His beloved (you and I), provided for us through making a covenant with us in the Mass and the Eucharist (Matthew 26:26-28). In the Jewish culture, the exchange of the chalice signifies the return of the husband-to-be. He would make this covenant to assure his beloved of his plans to leave and prepare for their wedding and the rooms in his father's house. Jesus did this too. He returned to His Father's House to prepare rooms for us, His Bride, and He promised He will return to take His beloved there.

"I am the bread of life. Whoever comes to me will never be hungry, and whoever believes in me will never be thirsty" (John 6:35). Men reflect the glory of God and are created in His image and likeness, hence the desire to provide as God provides.

Third Glorious Mystery – The Coming of the Holy Spirit

God is Covenant. I am secured.

We are Children of the Eternal Covenant. We are chosen in Christ and "marked with the seal of the promised Holy Spirit" (Ephesians 1:13).

Before Jesus returned to His Father in Heaven, He promised us the Counsellor (John 16:7) who would be our Guide on our journey in the path of Truth and Righteousness. Even "if we are faithless, he remains faithful – for he cannot deny himself" (2 Timothy 2:13), and God's Holy Spirit is God's faithfulness alive in us.

"The Spirit Song" by John Wimber is the song that I was inspired by as I reflected on this mystery. I encourage you to take this song too (you can find it on YouTube) as you pray and reflect on God's everlasting Covenant and love for us.

Fourth Glorious Mystery – The Assumption of Mary

God is the Way. I am directed.

We all desire a clear direction of where we are heading and we want to know where our destination may be. Jesus told us clearly, "I am the way, and the truth, and the life. No one comes to the Father except through me" (John 14:6). Mary, assumed to the highest Heaven, is the greatest example of someone who looked to Jesus as the Way to eternal life.

Saint John Paul II said, "The way Jesus shows you is not easy. Rather, it is like a path winding up a mountain. Do not lose heart! The steeper the road, the faster it rises towards ever wider horizons." After Jesus walked the steep path towards Calvary, we witnessed His Glorious Resurrection and this is the prize that has been won victoriously for us all. Mary, His Mother, walked closely with Him through this journey to Calvary and was later crowned by God as the Queen of Heaven.

It is then our choice whether we are to follow the Way, which leads to Eternity, Freedom, Truth and Life.

Fifth Glorious Mystery - The Crowning of Mary, Queen of Heaven

God is Patience. I am embraced.

We, the Church, are the bride of Christ, and He is the Bridegroom. Therefore, as we take on this crown as the bride, Jesus promises His patience for us. He promises to hold our hands in good and in bad, in joy and in sorrow, and in health and in sickness. He will embrace us.

As in the third sorrowful mystery, the Crowning of

Thorns, Jesus took on this Crown so that we could one day receive the glorious throne in Heaven. This promise is realised as we see the crowning of Mary as the Queen of Heaven.

This calls for our perseverance to holiness. Jesus knows our human nature and He promises to be patient with us until we surrender the prickly crown and receive this throne of glory.

Final Reflections

I pray that these reflections will assure you of your significance as the person God has created you to be. You were all planned to be united in love with Him before the foundation of the world was laid (Ephesians 1:4). God desires greatness in you as He Himself is a Great God. I also pray that as you reflect on these mysteries, your love for the Kingdom will grow each day and that it will manifest gloriously wherever you may be.

"Before I formed you in the womb
I knew you,
and before you were born
I consecrated you;
I appointed you a prophet to the nations"
(Jeremiah 1:5).

How to Pray the Rosary[2]

As you pray your Rosary beads, there is a prayer for each bead, and this quick guide will help you along the way!

- Pray, 'In the Name of the Father, and the Son, and the Holy Spirit. Amen."

- Holding the Crucifix on your Rosary, begin with the Apostle's Creed:

> I believe in God, the Father almighty,
> Creator of heaven and earth,
> and in Jesus Christ, His only Son,
> our Lord,
> who was conceived by the Holy Spirit,
> born of the Virgin Mary,
> suffered under Pontius Pilate,
> was crucified, died and was buried;
> He descended into hell;
> on the third day He rose again from the dead;
> He ascended into heaven,
> and is seated at the right hand of God the Father almighty;
> from there He will come to judge the living and the dead.
> I believe in the Holy Spirit,

---

[2] Adapted from the YouCat (28, 480, 481, 511)

the holy catholic Church
the communion of saints,
the forgiveness of sins,
the resurrection of the body,
and the life everlasting.
Amen.

- Holding the first bead, pray the 'Our Father'

Our Father, who art in heaven,
hallowed by Thy Name,
Thy kingdom come,
Thy will be done
on earth as it is in heaven.
Give us this day our daily bread,
and forgive us our trespasses,
as we forgive those who trespass against us
and lead us not into temptation,
but deliver us from evil.
Amen.

- Pray the 'Hail Mary' prayer three times on the next three beads:

Hail, Mary,
full of grace,
the Lord is with you.
Blessed are you among women,
and blessed is the fruit of your womb, Jesus.
Holy Mary, Mother of God, pray for us sinners,
now and at the hour of our death.
Amen.

- Pray the 'Glory Be' prayer on the next bead:

> Glory be to the Father,
> and to the Son,
> and to the Holy Spirit,
> as it was in the beginning,
> is now and ever shall be,
> world without end.
> Amen.

- After this, each of the five decades has one 'Our Father', then the 'Hail Mary' prayer ten times, and a 'Glory Be'.

- Depending on the day of the week, there are different types of Mysteries to reflect on, and you can use this chapter to help you pray and think about them!

- To finish, pray 'In the Name of the Father, and of the Son, and of the Holy Spirit. Amen.'

Joyful Mysteries (Monday and Saturday)

1. **The Annunciation of the Archangel to Mary**
   God is Adventurer! I am adventurous!

2. **Mary's Visitation to Elizabeth**
   God is the Truth! I am true!

3. **The Birth of Jesus, the Messiah**
   God nurtures. I am nurtured.

4. **The Presentation in the Temple**
   God is Holy. I am holy.

5. **Finding the Boy Jesus in the Temple**
   God is Wisdom. I am wise.

The Luminous Mysteries (Thursday)

1. **The Baptism of the Lord**
   God is the Loving Father. I am His beloved child.

2. **The Wedding at Cana in Galilee**
   God is ever New. I am transformed.

3. **Jesus proclaims the Kingdom of God**
   God is the General. I am a warrior.

4. **The Transfiguration**
   God is Light. I shine.

5. **The Institution of the Eucharist**
   God is Communion. I am consumed.

The Sorrowful Mysteries (Tuesday and Friday)

1. **Jesus prays at the Garden of Gethsemane**
   God transcends. I am free.

2. **The Scourging at the Pillar**
   God is Protector. I am protected.

3. **The Crowning of Thorns**
   God is Beauty. I am beautiful.

4. **The Carrying of the Cross**
   God is Strength. I am strong.

5. **Jesus is Crucified.**
   God is Love. I am loved.

The Glorious Mysteries (Wednesday and Sunday)

1) **The Resurrection of Jesus**
   God is Life. I am alive.

2) **The Ascension of Jesus**
   God is the Provider. I have enough.

3) **The Coming of the Holy Spirit**
   God is Covenant. I am secured.

4) **The Assumption of Mary**
   God is the Way. I am directed.

5) **The Crowning of Mary, Queen of Heaven**
   God is Patience. I am embraced.

CHAPTER 5: SOUND CHECK – WORSHIP
Mia Swientek

Miriam is an artist who grew up in the ICPE Mission. She enjoys everything beautiful, a nice cup of coffee and long conversations with good friends. When you give her a book and good music she will not leave her room for the next couple of hours unless she smells sushi in the kitchen.

"The worst prison would be a closed heart" St John Paul II

One of my favourite movies is Tangled. The main character, Rapunzel, is a princess who was abducted from her parents by the evil Gothel when she was a baby because of her rejuvenating powers. Knowing nothing about this she grows up in a tower, believing that Gothel is her mother and she is just a random girl. Creative as she is, she finds numerous ways to entertain herself and is quite happy with her life. As the years pass, Rapunzel realizes that every year on her birthday thousands of floating lights appear in the sky, brighter than the stars. She starts to become really fascinated with them and decides that she wants to see them for real!

When selfish Gothel hears about this idea she forbids Rapunzel to ever leave the tower (the worst thing that could happen to her is that Rapunzel finds out who she really is...). Some time later the young thief Flynn Ryder ends up in the tower seeking refuge. He agrees to help Rapunzel to escape and to see the floating lights. She enters the adventure of her life and takes a long journey where she discovers the world for the first time. She finds out that her biological parents, the king and the queen, have been releasing paper lanterns every year on her birthday, hoping that she would return to them one day. They never gave up on her and it was worth it!

It was also really worth it that Rapunzel left the place she was used to in order to strive for something more fascinating. It took courage, it took sacrifice and it became the most important journey of her life! In the end she doesn't just get to see the floating lights and marry Flynn Ryder but most importantly she discovers her true identity as a princess and returns to her parents to one day rule the kingdom.

She had to make a **decision.** Would she stay in her secure tower (although it really only was a pretty prison)? Or would she follow that inward voice telling her that there was something out there that she **must** see even if it meant leaving behind what she had known so far?

God is calling you to **see** more and to **discover** more than you have known so far. He is inviting you on a journey today. He is the King who is calling you home!

This chapter will be about decisions, about worship, about God, about you, about beauty and about relationship. I pray that the words you read may bring you life and help you to get to know God and yourself more.

Loud and Quiet, Old and New, Fast and Slow

Depending on your background the word 'worship' stirs different pictures in you. What most of us associate 'worship' with is music or even a particular music style and one hour of singing songs in our youth groups. While it is great to sing songs that move our heart and have a catchy tune it is important to become aware that worship has nothing to do with the style, speed or the volume of a song and can't be limited to music. God is the one who created music and we are only the ones composing it. Worship is **far more** than one hour of singing the latest (or alternatively in some places the not-so-latest!) worship-hits and is not just for musicians.

The Latin word for worship is adōrātiō and means to **show a demonstration of respect or honour to someone or something.**

You've got a lovely smile! (You really do!)

You can show respect by your **words**: in most countries you wouldn't call your teacher by their first name, but 'Mr...' or 'Mrs...' for example. It shows a respect of their authority.

You can also honour somebody by your **actions**: when it is your friend's birthday and you sing them a song and give them a gift it shows that the person is important to you because you:

- remembered their birthday (or Facebook told you)

- did something to show the person that you are aware it is a special day

- found a way to express your gratitude for them

Words and actions are also a fruit of our thoughts and therefore what happens inside us is of major, pivotal, highest and crucial importance!

Honouring the people around us is wonderful and God loves it when we do that!

My friend **loves** food and I remember a time when we went to a place that sold pulled pork. The moment the juicy meat touched his taste buds he started exclaiming: "Oh my goodness! It's so good! They are geniuses here!"

Because he gets really loud when he is excited - and he was very excited - his praises about the perfect tenderness of the meat could be heard across the place. Although he didn't address the cook directly he still surely made that guy smile. **By praising the art of an artist we praise the artist, too.** When we encourage a person it is like saying: God you did well with your creation and you are a good Creator. I encourage you to find ways to express your gratitude and respect for the people you meet because how we speak to others really makes a difference! We can speak life (or not) by what we are saying (or not saying). When we show gratefulness to others, it also trains us to establish a culture of life in our words and changes the way we think about ourselves and others.

Yet there is a big difference between honouring people and worshipping God. When we honour people we acknowledge them for who they are and we express our respect for them. When we honour God we acknowledge Him for who He is and we express our respect for Him. Sounds the same? Both acknowledge someone for who they are and both express our respect according to their identity. That's where the distinction comes in, because God holds a unique position in the universe…

- God is God.

- And everyone else is not God.

- He is the Source of everything.

- He is our Saviour and has brought us from darkness into light.

- He is the Lord and Master of everything that exists.

- He is never-ending and merciful Love.

- He is the **only One** in whom we will find the "truth and happiness that we are searching for" (CCC, 27).

Therefore, God is the only one who deserves adoration.

For Catholics it is important to point out that we honour and love the Saints and Mary and our leaders in the Church, **but we don't worship them.** They are not God and they never will be.

Extraordinary God

God is alive, passionate and all-consuming, and He wants **all of you**!

"You shall love the Lord your God with **all** your heart, and with **all** your soul, and with **all** your strength, and with **all** your mind; and your neighbour as yourself" (Luke 10:27, emphasis added).

So many 'alls' in one sentence! That's pretty intense. God is making it quite obvious that He isn't interested in being a nice add-on to our lives. What He is asking of us here is that we give Him our heart completely: to surrender. Surrender isn't exactly the most popular word in today's culture. It sounds like defeat and submission and in our competitive world we learn never to give up, to win and to be successful. And yet surrender is at the core of worship.

95% is not enough. He loves and longs for every little part of you. He wants a life that honours Him in every aspect because He knows that when we worship and spend time with Him, we become like Him.

Let me take you on a journey to understand God's heart more.

Imagine this. You are carving a wooden miniature sword (like Aragorn's) and really enjoying it. As the hours pass and you keep cutting into the wood, what was once a plain trunk slowly takes shape. It isn't quite a sword yet but you are happy that you have finally started working on this project. For years you have been wanting to try it, but you were always too afraid that you just couldn't do it.

Today you braced yourself up and decided to try. You are really enjoying the new freedom. You love this moment. The smell of the wood and the scratchy sound of the knife have a wonderfully soothing effect on you and all you do is carve, carve, carve. Until suddenly you hear footsteps coming closer. Suddenly all your relaxation is gone and has been replaced by an awful anxiety that wraps its cold fingers around your heart. You are becoming very aware of the imperfections of your work, the uneven shape of the sword.

You get flashbacks of things people have said to you 'Haha, you call that art?', 'You? You really think that you can do that?', 'Just stick to maths'. Nobody was supposed to see this. What a stupid idea it was to even do this. Quickly you are trying to slide it under the table but it is too late.

A man enters the room, looking at you. This is even worse than you imagined! It is your uncle, a carpenter! The one whom you have been admiring since you were a little child. What is he even doing here?

While you have turned into a pillar of salt he walks up to you with a big smile and you hear him saying: 'Wow, what is that?' You aren't sure if you are hearing properly and while you are still wondering whether you fainted and started to dream he continues to talk, 'I am so proud of you for finally trying this out. From when you were little I noticed that you were very interested in wood and often I saw you watching me when I was working on a project in the workshop.'

'You, you saw me?' you hear yourself asking, feeling even more exposed. 'Oh yes I surely did', he smiled 'and I was waiting for the day when you would finally start carving yourself. It is something that is in you and I have seen it for a long time. I am overjoyed to see this gift come to life. If you want, I will help you to grow in this gift more.'

This uncle shows a lot of God's heart for you. Jesus has a really special way of seeing people. He sees dignity in somebody who is ashamed of himself and He sees greatness in the little beginnings.

That God wants all of you means that He also wants all the things about you that people don't like or don't believe in.

God wants all of you. He loves every part of you. Every minute detail about who you are. Looking at worship from this angle it becomes a miracle! **Our God, who is infinitely perfect and happy in Himself wants to see your expression of love because it means everything to Him.**

You are part of the big story He is writing and there is a role that only you can play! He wants all of you so He can shape you to be the person that He made, free from fear and sin so you can delight in Him and give your best without any pressure. When you allow Him to take the drivers' seat in your life, He can take you to wonderful places! It means to allow Him to be the Lord over your life and to be obedient to the things He is telling you to do, trusting that He knows best! That may mean that you have to give up something you have got used to and may not always be easy. But God is only telling you to give up things in order to give you something that is a million times better. And remember: You are not alone. You have been given the Holy Spirit who gives you the power to love God!

> "The more we let God take us over, the more truly ourselves we become - because He made us. He invented us. He invented all the different people that you and I were intended to be... It is when I turn to Christ, when I give up myself to His personality, that I first begin to have a real personality of my own" C.S. Lewis

Fear is a Liar

Usually one thing that keeps us from giving ourselves to God completely is that we are scared that He isn't trustworthy and that He wants to take away all the things we love from our life and just make us do boring things. When we see God in such a way it creates fear in us and it doesn't make us want to trust Him.

That's why it is really important to get to know Him more because the more you get to know Him the more you will discover **how very trustworthy He truly is** and the more you want to get to know Him more! He is not a brutal tyrant who forces us to worship Him, but He is a generous King who longs to be with His children, who gave everything to win you over by His love (Romans 8:32).

'God do you love me?' I once found myself asking God that question. I was sitting in my room and in my mind I knew that He did. It wasn't that something bad had happened, it was just a question that I wanted to ask Him. I guess it was just that I hadn't felt Him in a while and I didn't remember experiencing anything special.

Suddenly a little voice started whispering in my mind: "The very fact that you are here right now, breathing, asking the questions you are asking, means that I love you. Every millisecond that you are alive is because I am breathing life into you. If it weren't for my love you wouldn't exist.'

"Each of us is the result of a thought of God. Each of us is willed. Each of us is loved. Each of us is necessary"
Pope Benedict XVI

I learned two things that day:

The first thing I learned is something about God. God is the ever-present Creator. If it weren't for Him, nothing in creation would exist at all, and if He didn't decide to keep the world in existence...well there would be just...nothingness!

In the Catechism of the Catholic Church (a great book by the way!) it says:

> "To adore God is to acknowledge, in respect and absolute submission, the 'nothingness of the creature' who would not exist but for God" (CCC, 2097).

Secondly I realized that it is a such a **privilege** to exist! **That I exist means that I am wanted, treasured and loved by God**. God didn't have to make me, He choose to create me. I felt so grateful and just **wanted to** sit down at my piano and sing to Him because I was so happy to exist!

That's how worship works: God shows you how cool He is and how much he loves you and you respond 'God you are so awesome! Thank you!'

God doesn't force us to worship Him. I believe that if we truly see God for who He is we will want to respond to Him with all our being and we will want to express that.

God cares. He made you. He is always watching you. He takes care of every detail of your life. He has given you the ability to be glad. He has a good plan for your life. He forgives you when you do something wrong. He is patient with you. He will never give up on you.

Maybe while reading this you realized that there is an area in your life that you aren't trusting God with. If you would like to, you can give that to Him in a simple prayer.

But I am not Perfect

Another thing that can keep us from entering the fullness of what God has for us is that we think we need to be perfect to be accepted. That we try to have everything under control and try to be God! Actually trying to control everything really creates a lot of stress in our life. **God is God and we are not,** and if we try to be it will create a lot of chaos.

In our minds we know that we are human, but in our hearts? What emotions are stirred when we realize that there are things we can't do and when we realize that we are limited? There might be anger, fear, frustration, envy and self-pity. We might start to compare ourselves and think someone else is better. We wish we could do everything but we just can't. **And that's ok.** That we aren't able to do everything makes us dependent on God. It opens us up to relationships and ultimately that is what we are designed for and what really makes us happy!

Everybody is a Worshipper

Ever wondered what it would be like to be a frog? If not, that's totally ok and means you have less odd thoughts than I do! When I was younger I sometimes envied my guinea pigs when I had to go school in the morning because while I was trying to remember Latin words or understand Physics (and it never succeeded the state of trying) 'Fipsy' and 'Tipsy' just got to stay home (my brother and I were too young to realize that the name implied that the second guinea pig was given strange things to drink; we just thought it sounded cool when we called them both and it rhymed).

All they had to take care of was to eat, play, poop and sleep. After second thoughts I felt quite happy to be human because that meant I could actually do many different things. The life of an animal (the same goes for plants) doesn't offer much variety or freedom whereas humans were given **the amazing gift of choice!**

Like every creature there are a lot of things which you have been given which you didn't choose, like your family, your hair colour, your height, your gender and many other things that make you the unique person you are. Another gift is your ability to worship. The choice that we get to make is: what will we do with what we have been given?

Everybody worships something or someone. Why do fans go crazy (and I mean the really obsessed kind of crazy) about actors and why do rich people buy amounts of clothes that they will never be able to wear in a life-time? The anthropologist Ludwig Klages (anthropologists are people who study humans) states that humans have an inclination to worship. It is as natural as eating and drinking. **We have been created to worship God** and if we don't worship Him, we will start looking for other things to centre our lives around.

Often we aren't even very aware of these things that become the driving force in our life. We can centre our life around being cool, being fashionable, being smart, being talented, being famous; we can be controlled by fear and by pressure and constantly work hard to gain the approval of people. That is worship too. It's called worshipping idols, focusing on a creation rather than the Creator.

What is an idol? **Something becomes an idol when it is treated like God although it isn't.** That means that things that aren't bad in themselves can turn into something bad for us.

This can happen when I start believing that the person that I am so in love with will fulfil all my heart's desires and I start arranging all my time, thoughts and money around him or her. Or when I make 'being cool' the centre of my life and start doing things that I know aren't good just because I long to be accepted.

The terrible thing is that those things just can't make us happy. They might make us feel better for a short while but in the end they will leave us empty. God made us to worship Him and nothing and nobody else can take His place. When we worship God, He is pleased and we enter into our identity as a beloved child of His and we get the energy to do what He is calling us to do because He gives us the approval and the love that we need.

When we worship something that He created, no matter how good that thing may be, it will take all our energy and leave us empty because the thing/person was not made to be worshipped and we are not made to worship that thing. It will always demand more and more of us and maybe give us a short satisfaction of our desires but eventually it will break our hearts. That's how addictions operate. Alcohol, pornography, excessive work, sports, gaming...

Worshipping something/someone other than God simply isn't good for us.

St Augustine discovered this:

"You have made us for yourself, Lord, and
our hearts are restless
until they find rest in you"
(Check out Audrey Assad's
song 'Restless' on YouTube)

The question is not **whether** we will worship but **whom** we will worship.

No Matter What the Cost

I once heard a story of a Muslim guy who converted to Christianity. He lived in a country where he could be killed for doing this and the man who was going to baptise him said: 'Are you sure, you want to do this? You know, you might get killed for it'. The response of the Muslim guy gave me the shivers: 'You have never seen Jesus have you? If you had, you wouldn't be saying this to me.'

This man had met Jesus and there was something so beautiful and dazzling, powerful and alive in the Son of God that it took away all his fear and he was even ready to die for Him.

Jesus is the most wonderful man that has ever been alive. Think about the most fascinating people you have ever met. What was it that fascinated you about them? Take some time to write it down. Do you know that everything beautiful on earth is an expression of God's beauty? That means that Jesus is the summit of everything fascinating in perfection. There is nothing on earth better than Him. The more we **see** Him for who He is the more we will **worship Him**.

Ever heard of Dishwasher-Worship?

Everything (except for sin) you do can be an act of worship to God! You can worship God while you're playing soccer, while you are baking, while you are writing, dancing, singing, jumping or whatever comes to your mind!

Brother Lawrence, who lived in the 17th century had the very non-spiritual task of washing dishes in his monastery. In his book 'The Practice of the Presence of God', he writes that our sanctification (becoming holy) does not depend so much on what we do, as it does on doing our activities for God rather than for ourselves. While he was doing his ordinary work he was talking to God and he believed that we should be united with Him when we are involved in our daily activities, just as our prayers unite us with Him at a quiet time. He washed the dishes obediently, out of love for God.

Our attitude really matters. We might be the most spiritual looking person from the outside, doing all kinds of devotions and going to Mass every day, but what God really cares about is whether we are doing what we are doing out of love for Him and that can't be judged from the outside. What He really cares about is our heart (Mark 12:41-44).

To Worship God is to Speak the Language of Faith

Did you know that the Psalms are the longest book in the Bible? They are an expression of faith through the drama of life. David, who wrote most of them went through all sorts of things (like being bullied, being forgotten, being left alone, living in a cave, really screwing up badly, becoming a king, defeating a giant...) and throughout it all he expressed his faith in God! He believed that God was faithful and that He would be faithful till the end even if David really screwed up at times. David remained grateful even when his life looked really, really bad.

The message he was shouting was: Take courage! Hope in the Lord! I will praise Him still!

> "I will extol you, my God and King,
> and bless your name forever and ever.
> Every day I will bless you,
> and praise your name forever and ever.
> Great is the LORD,
> and greatly to be praised;
> his greatness is unsearchable."
> (Psalm 144:1-3 [145:1-3]).

Some years ago I made it my aim to make the language of praise my first language. I noticed that the language that is mostly spoken in the world is one of hopelessness and putting people down and I noticed that, depending on what movies I watched and which people I would hang out with, my language would change. I decided to intentionally learn the language of faith and David has been a great role model for me!

The Psalms are an awesome way to help us to find vocabulary to pray and to praise God. You can use a Psalm and use it for your time of prayer and make it your own. Soak in it, read it over and over again. You can even sing it out if you want to! I noticed that the more words I discover to describe God, the clearer my vision of Him has become and the more I want to express my worship for Him!

You could also try to find attributes for God from A-Z (and let me know which one you found for 'X'...). There are many ways for us to expand our vocabulary of faith. It could be through reading the Bible, listening to songs that describe God, spending time with people of faith or anything else that comes to mind!

The way we speak has an impact on us and I believe that for living this life of worship it is so important to speak a language of faith, hope, love and worship in every aspect of life. We want to worship God whole-heartedly and how we use our tongue plays a major role in our worship!

Sing, Sing, Sing!

There are times when we intentionally gather as a community of believers and take time to make music for the Lord and express our faith through songs. Hopefully, the following lines will help you to understand why God is calling us to sing to Him.

"The LORD, your God, is in your midst,
a warrior who gives victory;
he will rejoice over you with gladness,
he will renew you in his love;
he will exult over you with loud singing"
(Zephaniah 3:17).

God rejoices over you with songs! I love that! He is singing over you! God is there and He delights in you.

"...be filled with the Spirit, as you sing
psalms and hymns and spiritual songs

among yourselves, singing and making
melody to the Lord in your hearts"
(Ephesians 5:18-19).

Singing is a wonderful thing! It is wonderful when believers come together to sing about God's greatness and glory and splendour and beauty and majesty and goodness and kindness and truth and…you name it!

I am amazed with the abundance of songs that various people have written over the years to express their love for God. There is something really special about gathering as a group and intentionally taking time to sing to God. It means that we, as his redeemed children, as the Church, gather and proclaim that He is our God!

Have you ever noticed that for most people it is much easier to remember songs than to remember poems? We store an incredible amount of music in our brain and even if we haven't heard a song for a while we easily recognize it, even if it is years later. Music has a strong impact on individuals, groups and cultures. Just think of all the songs people sing during the FIFA World Cup and how engaged they can get.

Music is art. It influences us in a profound way. If you want to understand the core of a culture look at its art. Listen to its music. Wherever you go, you will find music and you will find songs and they carry a lot of emotion and express things in a very powerful way. Lately I read an article which stated that music can actually reduce chronic pain and even claimed that people who have visual areas in the brain which are affected after a stroke regain some of their visual attention when they listen to their favourite music! Music brings people together and shapes their worldview - either in a good or in a bad way.

The Bible begins with the poetry of Genesis which is sometimes also called the Hymn of Creation and ends with a couple of great songs of worship in the book of Revelation. Already in Genesis 4:21 the first musician is introduced: Jubal, the father of all who play the harp and the flute. Throughout Scripture, music is mentioned in at least 44 books. The Psalms are a whole book of songs. In the history of the Church, music has been an integral part of the faith in every corner of the globe. **God desires the songs of His people!**

"Let them thank the LORD
for his steadfast love,
for his wonderful works to humankind.
And let them offer thanksgiving sacrifices,
and tell of his deeds with songs of joy"
(Psalm 106:21-22 [107: 21-22]).

Music is a natural expression of joy. Whenever there is a party there is always music! That's one of the reasons why we play songs during Mass. We naturally express that we are celebrating Christ together! It is so beautiful and strengthening when we worship God together and mutually express thanksgiving, honour and petition as a unified body. There is power in singing songs and whenever we proclaim God's victory the atmosphere changes and the Lordship of Christ is declared over the place where we sing.

Leading Worship

Everybody is called to worship, remember! And what a worship leader does is to help people to worship. So if you are gonna worship God, it is important that you learn how to lead yourself in worship. And I also believe that everybody is called to be a worship leader.

The first person that you lead in worship is yourself!

So...what is worship leading all about?

A worship leader helps me/people to enter into the presence of God. Worship is responding to God, being in agreement with who God is.

So, what is really important is that the person leading knows the Father. Remember we spoke about Kind David earlier? Well, long before he even knew he was gonna be a king, he was a forgotten shepherd boy whom nobody cared about much and who was taking care of the sheep on the hillside all by himself. While he was there he wrote many songs for God and got to know Him more and more. Nobody was there to encourage him or to tell him that he was a great worship leader. And that didn't matter because he wrote his songs for God.

The time out there on the field was a very important time for David and prepared him to grow in his relationship with God. The time that you are in your room all alone, leading yourself in worship is precious and you **need that time**! True worship is developed in the secret place where nobody sees and it's just you and God (Matthew 6:6). Leading worship is a ministry of great humility, and humility means that you know who God is and who you are, and also that you are precious because you are loved by **Him**! It means that you know that you are a child of God and have been given a crown and during worship you lay that crown down at the altar because He is so worthy.

Maybe some of you are worship leaders in a broader sense or maybe you believe that God has put music on your heart and you might be leading groups of people in worship one day.

That is wonderful! God has a wonderful plan for you! Many of us musicians struggle with insecurity and we want people to like our music. Our generation is addicted to the need of approval. And this is very dangerous because the affirmation of people comes and goes. Leading worship is not about being the best musician on earth, playing the coolest guitar solos and the fanciest twirly piano melodies. Music can even become a distraction from true worship when we make worship leading about being cool in front of people. If that is true for you there is no need to put yourself down. Tell Jesus about it, receive His forgiveness and trust that the Holy Spirit will help you to become confident in the Father's love and continue to play and sing for Him. **Don't ever stop singing for Him!**

What sustains us is the affirmation of the Father!

The more you live out your identity as a son/daughter of

God, the more peaceful you will become when you lead worship. You will be able to minister **from** approval, rather than **for** approval. The closer you get to know God, the more you will also be able to share with others. Jesus spent His first 30 years on earth of growing in intimacy with the Father before He started His ministry. So I think it is ok for us to take a few years.

Some Practical Tips for Worship Leaders (And those to be)

1. Spend intentional time with God daily and make getting to know Him your **top priority**. You can ask Him: Father, what do you see when you look at me? Who am I to you?

2. Ask yourself this question: What kind of worship leader am I? There are three distinctions when we speak about worship-leaders:

a) You lead yourself in worship (everybody is called to do this!)

b) You serve as a worship leader for groups occasionally

c) Your whole life is committed to leading worship

Especially if you answered b) or c) my tip is: **practice your instrument**, and by the way your voice is an instrument, too!

Music is a great tool in worship leading and the more secure you feel in your musical skills the more you will be able to use your instruments for the glory of God. God still likes your worship even when you sing a wrong note, but for most people who aren't tone-deaf, it is usually quite distracting when there are too many wrong tunes. Also, let's just give our best to God, because He is worthy of it!

How much time do you want to give to worship leading in your life and how many hours of practice do you want to commit to? Write it down and stick to it!

"Sing to him a new song;
play skilfully on the strings,
with loud shouts"
(Psalm 32:3 [33:3]).

---

3. Learn and play songs by heart for the same reasons as above.

4. Listen to established worship leaders (like Matt Maher, Chris Tomlin and Matt Redman), observe and learn from them while remaining yourself and developing your own personal style. God desires **your** worship and you don't have to be anyone but you. He enjoys you and you are allowed to be unique and different in your worship style!

There are many different ways of leading worship and there isn't one right style. Be creative, use your gifts to glorify God and dare to try new things (maybe it's time for some of you to start writing your own songs?). Above all, remember that our aim as worship leaders is to lead people into the presence of God and to make room for Him to do whatever He wants to do.

God, You are worthy of our praises forever and we will sing to you, we will dance for you, we will jump for you!

CHAPTER 6: RED LIGHT – THE EUCHARIST
Father Tony Alex

Father Tony is a priest from India and is part of the Institute for World Evangelisation - ICPE Mission. In his free-time, if you don't find Father Tony playing sport, he will probably be watching Formula One!

What if I told you that Jesus Christ, in His person as flesh and not just a symbol of Him, is truly and fully present on this earth in some place right now, what would you do? Wouldn't you want to know where He is and if you could go and see Him, what would you do if you saw Him? Would you want to talk to Him, would you want to spend time just watching Him or would you just not care about Him and walk past Him saying to yourself "Hmmmm…He ain't no big dude." Or would you recognize Him as GOD, King and Saviour and go down on your knees or prostrate before Him to worship Him?

The reality is: He is here and the clue to find Him is the Red Light. As you walk into every Catholic Church or Chapel all over the world you will find a Red Light signalling He is present. When you spot the Red Light, next to it you will find a gold or silver plated or ornamented box like structure called a tabernacle. In every tabernacle in every Catholic Church around the globe, Jesus is fully and truly present in Body, Blood, Soul and Divinity in the form of the Eucharist. The

Eucharist is not a symbol or a sign or a representation, but it is Jesus Christ fully, really and truly present.

Thomas Merton a famous Trappist Monk and modern mystic wrote an autobiography called "The Seven Storey Mountain" which became one of the most famous books ever written about a man's search for faith and peace. In it he writes that when he was 10 years old, in the quaint little French town of St. Antonin, he was attracted to the local Church, and in his description about the Church he writes:

"I did not even know who Christ was, that He was God. I had not the faintest idea that there existed such a thing as the Blessed Sacrament. I thought churches were simply places where people got together and sang a few hymns. And yet now I tell you, you who are now what I once was, unbelievers, it is that Sacrament, and that alone, the Christ living in our midst, and sacrificed by us, and for us and with us, in the clean and perpetual Sacrifice, it is He alone Who holds our world together, and keeps us all from being poured headlong and immediately into a pit of our eternal destruction. And I tell you there is a power that goes forth from that Sacrament, a power of light and truth, even into hearts of those who have heard nothing of Him and seem to be incapable of belief."

Jesus Christ is alive and is among us in the form of the

Eucharist. As Catholics we are privileged to have this real presence of God celebrated and sacrificed every day that brings the reality of God to us in a very human and tangible way. It is the Eucharist that is the Source and Summit of all Christian life and Worship. Now this may seem all too high and theological and beyond your grasp so let's get to understanding this in a simpler way by asking some basic questions.

How does this all come about? How does Jesus take the form of bread called the Eucharist?

It all happens or comes about with the celebration of the Eucharist or what we commonly refer to as Holy Mass. It is at every Mass that the greatest of miracles takes place where the bread and wine become the Body and Blood of Christ.

The Lord Jesus, on the night before He suffered on the cross, shared one last meal with His disciples. During this meal our Saviour instituted the sacrament of His Body and Blood. He did this in order to bring about the sacrifice of the Cross throughout the ages and to entrust to the Church (His Spouse) a memorial of His death and resurrection. As the Gospel of Matthew tells us:

> "While they were eating, Jesus took a loaf of bread, and after blessing it he broke it, gave it to his disciples, and said, 'Take, eat; this is my body.' Then he took a cup, and

> after giving thanks he gave it to them,
> saying, 'Drink from it, all of you; for this is
> my blood of the new covenant, which is
> poured out for many for the forgiveness of
> sins.'" (Matthew 26:26-28; cf. Mark 14:22-
> 24, Luke 22:17-20, 1 Corinthians 11:23-25)

Recalling these words of Jesus, the Catholic Church professes that, in the celebration of the Eucharist, bread and wine become the Body and Blood of Jesus Christ through the power of the Holy Spirit and the instrumentality of the priest. The priest acts "in persona Christi" which means in the person of Christ, and performs the sacrifice.

Is it Jesus and is it His real presence in flesh and blood?

If you're struggling with this concept, you're not alone. The apostles had a hard time with this teaching too, but Jesus wouldn't budge. He insisted that He was going to give us His true flesh and blood to eat and drink, not just symbols. Check out what's given in the Bible in John, chapter 6. Jesus said:

> "I am the living bread that came down
> from heaven. Whoever eats of this bread
> will live forever; and the bread that I will
> give for the life of the world is my

flesh...for my flesh is true food and my blood is true drink" (John 6:51-55).

Over the centuries there were many people who had this same question and doubted. There were even many priests who did not believe in this real presence, one such priest was Peter of Prague. In 1263, Peter stopped at Bolsena (in Italy) while on a pilgrimage to Rome. He is described as being a pious priest, but one who found it difficult to believe that Christ was actually present in the consecrated Host. While celebrating Holy Mass above the tomb of St. Christina (located in the church named for this martyr), he had barely spoken the words of Consecration when blood started to seep from the consecrated Host and trickle over his hands onto the altar. It is said that Pope Urban IV was prompted by this miracle and instituted the feast of Corpus Christi, which is celebrated in the third week after the feast of the Ascension.

There are hundreds of other such occurrences where the bread and wine has turned into the visible Body and Blood at the celebration of the Mass. The miracle of Lanciano (in Italy) is the first, and many believe it is the greatest Eucharistic Miracle recorded and analyzed in the history of the Catholic Church. This wondrous event took place in the 8th century A.D. in the little Church of St. Legontian, as a divine response to a Basilian monk's doubt about Jesus' Real Presence in the Eucharist.

During Holy Mass, after the consecration, the host was changed into live Flesh and the wine was changed into live Blood, which coagulated (became semi-solid) into five globules, irregular and differing in shape and size. The Host-Flesh, as can be very distinctly observed even today, is light brown and appears rose-colored when lit up from the back. The Blood is coagulated and has an earthy colour. Since 1574 various investigations were conducted. In 1970-71 and taken up again partly in 1981 there took place a scientific investigation by the most illustrious scientist Prof. Odoardo Linoli, eminent Professor in Anatomy and Pathological Histology and in Chemistry and Clinical Microscopy. He was assisted by Prof. Ruggero Bertelli of the University of Siena. The analyses were conducted with absolute and unquestionable scientific precision and they were documented with a series of microscopic photographs. These analyses sustained the following conclusions:

- The Flesh is real Flesh. The Blood is real Blood.

- The Flesh and the Blood belong to the human species.

- The Flesh consists of the muscular tissue of the heart.

- In the Flesh we see present in section: the myocardium, the endocardium, the vagus nerve and also the left ventricle of the heart for the large thickness of the myocardium.

- The Flesh is a 'heart' complete in its essential structure.

- The Flesh and the Blood have the same blood-type: AB (the blood-type identical to that which Professor Baima Bollone uncovered in the Holy Shroud of Turin).

All this proved without doubt that it was the flesh and blood of Jesus. There are tons of other cool miracles to help us believe that the Eucharist is the real presence of Jesus, check out www.therealpresence.org.

There seems to be something mysterious about it, how can I understand this better?

Yes, it may seem mysterious because the presence of Jesus Christ in the Eucharist is a 'mystery.' The word 'mystery' is commonly used to refer to something that escapes the full comprehension of the human mind. In the Bible, however, the word has a deeper and more specific meaning, for it refers to aspects of God's plan of salvation for humanity, which has already begun but will be completed only with the end of time. In ancient Israel, through the Holy Spirit God revealed to the prophets some of the secrets of what he was going to accomplish for the salvation of His people (cf. Amos 3:7; Isaiah 21:28; Daniel 2:27-45).

Likewise, through the preaching and teaching of Jesus, the mystery of 'the kingdom of God' was being revealed to His disciples (Mark 4:11-12). St. Paul explained that the mysteries of God may challenge our human understanding or may even seem to be foolishness, but their meaning is revealed to the People of God through Jesus Christ and the Holy Spirit (cf. 1 Corinthians 1:18-25, 2:6-10; Romans 16:25-27; Revelations 10:7). The Eucharist is a mystery because it participates in the mystery of Jesus Christ and God's plan to save humanity through Christ. We should not be surprised if there are aspects of the Eucharist that are not easy to understand, for God's plan for the world has repeatedly surpassed human expectations and human understanding (cf. John 6:60-66). For example, even the disciples did not at first understand that it was necessary for the Messiah to be put to death and then to rise from the dead (cf. Mark 8:31-33, 9:31-32, 10:32-34; Matthew 16:21-23, 17:22-23, 20:17-19; Luke 9:22,43-45, 18:31-34). Furthermore, any time we speak of God we need to keep in mind that our human concepts never entirely grasp God. We must not try to limit God to our understanding, but allow our understanding to be stretched beyond its normal limitations by God's revelation.

What does this mystery of the Eucharistic Jesus in flesh and blood mean for me?

At Holy Mass when we receive the Eucharist, Jesus' Body and Blood under the appearance of bread and wine (just like at the Last Supper), we are renewing our covenant with God. We are reconfirming our promise to God to live out our end of the relationship.

A covenant, in this context, is a type of relationship. It is the type of relationship that God has always had with His people, whereby each party mutually agrees to something. God loves us endlessly and infinitely. God forgives us endlessly and infinitely. Our mutual response to God is to love Him as much as we can even though our love is finite. Our response is to obey God and receive His freely given grace to help bring the Kingdom of God here on Earth.

When we receive the Eucharist at each Mass we are making that promise to God that we will hold up our end of the covenant. We are also unifying ourselves to God and to the other members of the Church through the Body of Christ.

The whole purpose of Eucharistic celebration then is to worship God, unite ourselves with the sacrifice of Jesus, and to elevate our lives to a life with God. Out of this relationship with God we only get out what we put into it; God's grace can only work in our lives if we are open to receiving it.

How can I benefit from this great gift of the Eucharistic Lord?

The simple but yet most profound and powerful way is to partake of this Bread daily and spend time worshipping Him in Adoration.

Daily Bread: The Eucharist is the Source and Summit of Christian life; the strength we need to live our lives fruitfully and joyfully. Go to Him. I often have heard people say Mass is boring... I used to think that Mass was boring too and out of fear or to please my folks I would go for Mass every Sunday. I had a complete turnaround after I discovered Jesus in the Eucharist. When I partake of the Eucharist now, I feel Him and am moved in a powerful way. For years now I have understood that the Eucharist is the source of everything and I just cannot afford to miss out on Jesus daily. I have come to realize that Mass is not just about fulfilling an obligation but it is that great mystery from which I draw strength, grace, courage, wisdom and understanding. Then to think of it as Jesus who came down from heaven and humbled Himself to take human flesh about two thousand years ago, today He becomes present to us in the form of bread so we can take Him into our very own body! This is awesome! We become walking tabernacles. Why not try to go for Mass daily, not just on Sundays; and when you walk up to receive the Eucharist, be aware of the presence of Jesus. May you worthily and humbly receive Him, giving Him all the worship, honour and reverence!

Adoration: What's that you may ask? It's the totally awesome privilege that we have, to be in front of our God truly present in the Blessed Sacrament (the Eucharistic Bread) and pray. The priest exposes the Eucharist in a beautiful gold stand called a monstrance so we can gaze upon Him and worship Him and soak up the rays of grace! It truly rocks! It is like spending your time before the Love of your life and being able to talk about everything you want. Your joys and sorrows, excitement and worries, questioning and receiving answers, and at the end of it you can go back with a great assurance of being loved immensely. If the Blessed Sacrament is not in sight, you can sit before a tabernacle and you can open the eyes of your heart to see Him and be present with Him. St. Catherine Laboure sums it up beautifully:

"Whenever I go to the chapel, I put myself in the presence of our good Lord, and I say to Him, 'Lord, I am here. Tell me what You would have me to do'...And then, I tell God everything that is in my heart. I tell Him about my pains and my joys, and then I listen. If you listen, God will also speak to you, for with the good Lord, you have to both speak and listen. God always speaks to you when you approach Him plainly and simply."

Take time every week to spend at least an hour before the Eucharistic Lord and believe me in a month, you and the people around you will notice a marked difference in your life for the better.

Draw me close to You!

Whenever you see a Red Light from now on, whether it be at a traffic signal or on your home appliances, on communication towers or emergency signals, let it remind you of the great mystery of Jesus Christ, "through whom are all things and through whom we exist" (1 Corinthians 8:6). He is really and fully present to us today in the form of the Eucharist and is ever inviting you to draw close to Him.

CHAPTER 7: WEAPON TRAINING – THE BIBLE
Lizzie Ambrose and Lewis Dowle

Swordsmanship

I have a friend who collects swords. Lots of swords. Anything from Samurai swords (three of varying sizes) to King Arthur's sword, Aragorn's sword, and even a lightsabre! He has them displayed in his room as his prized possessions. We just hope no burglar tries to break into his room!

> "Indeed, the word of God is living and active, sharper than any two-edged sword, piercing until it divides soul from spirit, joints from marrow; it is able to judge the thoughts and intentions of the heart" (Hebrews 4:12).

God's Word is alive. It a weapon that we can carry with us. **But also carry inside us.** God's Word is powerful, it is by His spoken Word that our world came into existence"

> "Then God said, 'Let there be light'; and there was light" (Genesis 1:3).

God spoke and things happened. Correction: **God speaks and things happen.**

If we were in Medieval Times and needed to fight as a knight in shining armour, we wouldn't be a terribly good one if we didn't have a sword! For thousands of years the sword was man's weapon of attack and defence. St Paul knew this when he wrote:

"Take the helmet of salvation,
and the sword of the Spirit,
which is the word of God"
(Ephesians 6:17, emphasis added).

This chapter is a visit to the armoury. We are going to kit ourselves out for battle, but armour is only of value if we have a weapon. So let's take up the sword of the Spirit, the Word of God

A Call to Action

A few years ago I was at a church Summer Camp. We used to sing a collection of songs, ones with catchy melodies and fun actions, but also a deeper message. One of them went like this:

"Your **Word**, Lord, is a lamp unto my feet,
And a light unto my path"

Another went like this:

"The **Name** of the Lord
is a strong tower,
the righteous run in to,
and they are saved"

At the time the words didn't really make that deep an impression on me. But over time, these words have often been my prayer and become a part of me. Beyond the catchy melody and the fun actions, these songs were Bible verses (God's Word) which over time took root in my heart (Psalm 118:105 [119:105]; Proverbs 18:10).

God speaks to us. He writes things on our heart. We need to hear God's Word.

"So faith comes from what is heard,
and what is heard comes
through the word of Christ"
(Romans 10:17).

When God spoke at the beginning of Creation, He spoke Creation into being. We too need to hear the Word of God and speak it over our lives. Because it is alive, it will transform us or the situations we face. God's Word can never come back empty:

"...so shall my word
be that goes out from my mouth;
it shall not return to me empty,
but it shall accomplish
that which I purpose,
and succeed in the thing
for which I sent it"
(Isaiah 55:11).

And it doesn't matter if we learn to speak the Bible verse from Little Church songs or learning verses whilst lifting weights.

"My child, be attentive to my words;
incline your ears to my sayings. Do not let
them escape from your sight; keep them
within your heart. For they are life to those
who find them, and healing to all their
flesh" (Proverbs 4:20-22).

The songs I used to sing at the camp have become etched on my heart. They are a part of who I am.

"write them on the tablet of your heart"
(Proverbs 7:3).

In St John's Gospel, he writes:

"And the Word became flesh and lived among us, and we have seen his glory, the glory as of a father's only son, full of grace and truth" (John 1:14).

When we speak God's Word, we are speaking words of Truth, Life, Healing, Forgiveness, Favour, Mercy, Protection, Guidance and so much more over our lives. **Jesus is the Word.** The 'Word became flesh': the Word became human.

Like a sponge, we need to soak up the Word, we need to absorb it. We need to speak it over our lives. Study it. Repeat and repeat and repeat it until we **see** it in our hearts and minds.

Saint Mother Teresa said this:

"The longest journey that a man must take is the eighteen inches between his head to his heart."

Not only knowing the words in our minds, **but believing them in our hearts.** Being open to the Word as we speak it over our lives opens up the floodgates of the Holy Spirit.

A Call to Mission

The ICPE (International Catholic Programme for Evangelisation) Mission's statement is: **'To know Christ and make Him known'.** Before we can evangelise, we need to know Christ, we need to know His love for us. When we study the Word, we are encountering the Living God. The Creator of the universe is speaking to us and we enter into a relationship with Him.

Imagine your friends trying to set you up with someone. Say there's this guy called Jed. They think he's perfect for you. He is intelligent, honest, sincere and six-foot two in height. When he isn't at the church praying for his future wife, he is probably at the gym working out. He is kind, caring, loves animals and making people smile.

These all sound great things in a guy. But here's the problem. You need to meet him in person. You can't make your mind up about a person you have never met. This can be true in our relationship with Jesus as well. Only by meeting Jed will we come to know the person. By reading God's Word we come to know Jesus. St Jerome wrote this:

"Ignorance of Scripture
is ignorance of Christ"

We could also say: **the more we know the Scriptures, the more we know Christ**.

'It is Written'

When the Word of God takes root in our hearts there is power. No force can stop God's Word coming to pass and His promises being fulfilled.

"...you know in your hearts and souls, all of you, that not one thing has failed of all the good things that the LORD your God promised concerning you; all have come to pass for you, not one of them has failed"
(Joshua 23:14)

How we respond to challenges, to temptations and setbacks can show our character and who/what we place our trust in. When temptations come, do we say 'Yes please! I would like two to takeaway', or do we reject the temptation? And if we choose to reject the temptation, how do we turn our back to it? As always, Jesus is our example.

After being baptised in the Jordan river by St John the Baptist, Jesus spent 40 days in the desert. There He was tempted by the devil on three occasions. Jesus was like us in all things but sin. He even faced temptations like you and I. But Jesus knew there was power in Scripture, power in the Word of God, so for each temptation He replied with 'It is written' and quoted Scripture.

> "Again, the devil took him to a very high
> mountain and showed him all the
> kingdoms of the world and the splendour;
> and he said to him, 'All these I will give
> you, if you will fall down and worship me.'
> Jesus said to him, 'Away with you, Satan!
> for it is written,
> "Worship the Lord your God,
> and serve only him."'
> Then the devil left him, and suddenly
> angels came and waited on him"
> (Matthew 4:8-11).

What Jesus does here is what we can do likewise. It's a little like this: **Stop, Play, Repeat.**

Temptations are going to come. When Jesus was tempted by the devil, He **stopped** the temptation with Scripture. There is huge power in Jesus' Words, 'It is written'. We too can follow Jesus' example by quoting Scripture. This is not always easy, but with God's grace it is possible.

If there is a really annoying catchy song (likely a Carly Rae one...), if you stop the track, the tune is still going to be in your mind. If there is just silence, we could have the song on an endless loop in our head. We have to **play** a new track. One which is possibly even more catchy (enter Taylor Swift)!

If our thoughts are not in the right place, we can change the track and replace it with Scripture. A Word of God. Just as Jesus replied with the opposite, so too can we do the same. If we feel discouraged, we can put on the track John 3:16:

"For God so loved the world that he gave
his only Son, so that everyone who
believes in him may not perish but may
have eternal life"

If we ever find ourselves lonely, let's put on
Deuteronomy 31:6:

"Be strong and bold; have no fear or dread
of them, because it is the LORD
your God who goes with you;
he will not fail you or forsake you."

Or if we feel flat, put on the catchy track of Romans 8:1:

"There is therefore now no condemnation
for those who are in Christ Jesus."

Maybe someone or something is intimidating us, let's put
on 2 Timothy 1:7:

"for God did not give us a spirit of
cowardice, but rather a spirit of power and
of love and of self-discipline."

Perhaps you may be struggling with believing in the

Eucharist? Well we've got to put on John 6:55:

"for my flesh is true food and
my blood is true drink."

Or maybe you feel anxious about your future? Know God has a plan for you and He says so in Jeremiah 29:11:

"For surely I know the plans I have for
you, says the LORD, plans for your
welfare and not for harm, to give you a
future with hope."

Or if we're facing a really hard Maths test, Philippians 4:13 is particularly catchy!

"I can do all things through him who
strengthens me."

If God's Word is entrenched in us, it is part of us. It becomes a natural response. If we really understood the power of Jesus' Name and the power of His Word, Jesus could use us to do 'even greater things' - **to give Him glory** (John 14:12)!

The step after this is **repeat**. Just keep it up. If the temptation comes, change the track. Keep repeating the **new** track until you can't get it of your head! It is a life-long process.

We need to be pro-active, we need to make the move, and the Holy Spirit gives us the strength we need.

"Therefore the LORD waits to be gracious with you; therefore he will rise up to show mercy to you" (Isaiah 30:18).

Walkie-Talkie

Imagine there's a guy who is good at nearly everything. Whatever he sets his mind to, he is amazing at. His only problem is that he doesn't last long in whatever he gets into! First it's rugby, then it's the guitar, soon after it's kayaking...It is very easy for all of us to start things but to then go head-over-heels in too quickly and we soon lose interest.

Just as a boat out at sea needs an anchor, so too do we need Jesus as our Anchor. We when place our trust in the Word of God, when we choose God as our Anchor, we aren't swayed by the tides, winds or currents. We find a peace and a hope.

"We have this hope, a sure and steadfast
anchor of the soul"
(Hebrews 6:19, emphasis added).

We start by knowing, loving and breathing God's Word in our everyday. With God's Word, it is a journey. **Start small**. Find a Bible verse that speaks to you. **Say it, then repeat it again and again.**

> "All scripture is inspired by God and is useful for teaching, for reproof, for correction, and for training in righteousness" (2 Timothy 3:16).

Scripture is inspired by God. It teaches us. It guides us. It changes us. It transforms us. Maybe you've seen the Transformers movies. Inside each of us is great potential. We are much more than just what society sees in us. We are more than just a car. We can be like a transformer. We can turn into a robot. Sort of. In fact, something much more exciting than a robot: **we become who God made us to be**. St Catherine of Sienna once said:

> "Be who God meant you to be and you will set the world on fire."

And not in the sense of robots setting fire to things...We will set the world on fire with God's love. Share His message of hope. Share the joy of His plans for each of us.

Often at the end of Bibles you'll find verses to use for particular situations. Just like a first-aid kit in battle. You will see pages of verses which are all about 'Thanksgiving' or

'Courage' or 'Humility'. These can be a great place to begin.

Jesus knows that little by little He can entrust us with more to give Him glory. He knows the Word sets us free and on fire for Him. And He is the Word! Here are five ways to help all of us go deeper in the Word.

Equip Yourself

B - Believe the Word. Jesus said in three Gospel accounts how 'Heaven and earth will pass away, but my words will not pass away' (Matthew 24:35; cf. Mark 13:31, Luke 21:33). We need to believe the Word. As we do it sparks something inside us. It sparks a hope.

"Truly I tell you, if you say to this mountain, 'Be taken up and thrown into the sea,' and if you do not doubt in your heart, but believe that what you say will come to pass, it will be done for you" (Mark 11:23).

When we believe, it is like putting a key in a door. It makes things happen.

I - Immerse yourself in the Word. They say with learning a language that the best way to do so is to 'immerse' yourself in it. This means living in the country, living with people who speak the lingo, putting yourself outside of your comfort zone in order to develop the skill. We can also think of immersion like when we swim. When we go fully into the water, from top to toe, we *immerse* ourselves in it. Our whole body is in the water.

To immerse ourselves in the Word of God is to surround ourselves with it. To choose carefully what we read, talk about, watch, think about, listen to. It is bringing God into our everyday.

Our Church has a rich and deep heritage of love for the Word of God. Every single day of the calendar year there are daily readings of Scripture for different hours of the day. Every single Catholic Church across the globe will be reading and listening to those same words which we can read in the Divine Office (or can find online at: www.usccb.org/bible/readings/). There are amazing initiatives like the Soul Survivor 'New Testament in a Year' which splits the New Testament into daily bite-size pieces. There may also be a great Bible study group to be apart of near you, maybe within your Church or school.

B - Base your life on the Word. God's Word is stable. Jesus is the Rock on whom we build our life. God's Word doesn't change with society and it isn't a buffet we choose only the things we like from. It is the eternal Word of God:

"The LORD exists forever; your word is
firmly fixed in heaven"
(Psalm 118:89 [119:89]).

It is easy to base our lives on material things and it is something we all easily do. The responses the world teaches seem 'quick-fixes' to our problems. But anyone who's made anything out of crafts or written computer programmes will know that a compromise here and a quick-fix there will only make things harder in the long run. God's Word may not become a habit instantly, but brushing your teeth used not to be either (and still may not be...)! We can change our patterns, we can change our whole way of living. This requires swimming against the current, going against the easy option. But when we base our lives on the Word, we will flourish like the palm tree (Psalm 91:13 [92:12])!

L - Love and Live the Word. What would you bring with you to a desert island? If you were allowed three things what would they be? The Bible is a great start. For a while in my life I wouldn't read the Bible that often, because if I were to read anything Christian, I found other books more interesting and easier to read. A couple of years ago this was flipped on its head. I suddenly had a passion for God's Word during my gap-year; it was a deep love for my Bible which I had never had before. We can ask the Holy Spirit to give us a love for the Word. It is easy to get out of the habit, trust me I know, but just as we need to keep adding wood to keep the fire going, so too we can fan the flame by immersing ourselves in

God's Word.

E - #Evangelise with the Word. By the way we live our lives, we are being a witness to God. St Francis of Assisi said:

"Preach the Gospel at all times and when necessary use words."

Our lives are the primary form of witness. But when we do use words, we can use them for God's glory. We are the social media generation. As young people we have huge potential to use social media to bring God's love to others. It is now easier than ever to share God's Word. We can share a Bible verse on Facebook. Retweet an inspiration quote. We could post a photo of God's Creation on Instagram. Maybe share our Christian playlist from Spotify with a friend. Or recommend a Christian video from YouTube to someone. As the Bible says:

"Finally, beloved, whatever is true, whatever is honourable, whatever is just, whatever is pure, whatever is pleasing, whatever is commendable, if there is any excellence and if there is anything worthy of praise, think about these things" (Philippians 4:8).

So whatever is honourable, pure, excellent, worthy of

praise: **share it.**

Lizzie Ambrose and Lewis Dowle like your status.

CHAPTER 8: THEOLOGY OF THE BODY FOR HER

Josipa Jurić Zelenika

Josipa is a final year student, an active member of the university's Catholic Society and a Salesian at heart. She's passionate about Theology of the Body, youth ministry, women's ministry, rosaries (never enough), praise and worship, daisies, Star Wars, Disney and her home country Croatia. She enjoys smiling, listening to music and breaking out in song whenever she can. You may hear her bursting into "I have decided to follow Jesus" or a random Croatian song at the Catholic Chaplaincy while baking cookies...

Do you remember your first day few days in a new environment? Do you remember the most common questions you were asked on those days – what's your name? Where are you from? What do you study? What year are you in? By the end of my first week at university, whenever I met someone new, I blurted out an automatic answer containing all the relevant info I wanted people to know: name, place of birth, age, family life, favourite colour, favourite cheesy 90s song (yes, Macarena) all the 'important' stuff, of course.

Fastfoward a few months, 'this important stuff' simply wasn't enough. The answers I gave were not answering some big questions: Who am I? Where do I belong? What am I supposed to be doing? Perhaps you've felt this way. I'm here to tell you, you're definitely not alone! As humans we have a deep curiosity to know where people come from, to know who they are and what they do. We have an even deeper desire to know who **we** are, where we come from and where we belong, and what we're supposed to be doing.

However, we too often stop at the superficial – the easy information that will only temporarily satisfy both our, and the desire of others, to really know each other – you know, the 'important stuff' like who your favourite Disney princess is (Cinderella, obviously). As much as this little piece of information is entertaining and a part of me and maybe even a part of you, it won't really tell either of us who we really are, so I want to take you back to the beginning, and I don't mean to the day you came into this world. I mean way back to the beginning –when woman was created! I want to remind you who you really are and the glorious things God has imagined for you as a woman.

In The Beginning

Remember the story of how God created the world in 7 days (well 6, God knew to kick back and relax on day 7)? He creates all these awesome things: day, night, water, land, plants, animals and finally, He decides to make man:

> "Then God said, 'Let us make humankind
> in our image, according to our likeness;
> and let them have dominion over the fish
> of the sea, and over the birds of the air,
> and over the cattle, and over the cattle, and
> over all the wild animals of the earth, and
> over every creeping thing that creeps upon
> the earth…God saw that everything that
> he had made, and indeed, it was very good.
> And there was evening and there was
> morning, the sixth day" (Genesis 1:26-27,
> 31)

He creates you and I in His own image and likeness, and He says 'it was very good'. This is really important so remember it for later!

In the second account of Genesis, God makes Adam, and he's just chillin' in this awesome garden (Eden) God has made especially for him – literally, the happiest place on earth. But soon Adam realizes that there's no one else like him – all these animals God has created are great, but definitely not his type. He feels like something is missing. God knows this and says "It is not good that the man should be alone" (Genesis 2:18), and here woman, Eve, comes in:

> "So the LORD God caused a deep
> sleep to fall upon the man, and he slept;
> then he took one of his ribs and closed up
> its place with flesh. And the rib that the
> LORD God had taken from the man he

made into a woman and brought to her to
the man"
(Genesis 2:21-22).

Adam was so astounded and amazed by this creature, he called out to her and said "This at last is bone of bones and flesh of my flesh" (Genesis 2:23). This may sound like a strange exclamation to you, but there are actually beautiful interpretations of what was really meant by a 'rib' in Genesis. You see, the 'rib' woman was made from has a much deeper meaning than simply being a body part. For ancient peoples, the most important part of man's body was his heart – for them it contained the very life of man – simply because if the heart stopped beating, man would be dead. The rib then, which surrounds the heart, was understood as a crucial part of life – it was its guardian or its keeper. So when we say woman was made of 'rib', we are actually saying that woman is the guardian of life. We are in essence the original bodyguards! This instantly makes sense because of our innate life-bearing and life-giving capabilities. We were not made of man's rib because we are less worthy but because we were given a great gift of guardianship in the form of both physical and spiritual motherhood.

The original word for 'rib' also translates as 'side', meaning that woman was made out of Adam's side or of half-of-Adam. This means that men and women are made of the same 'stuff' and that we are equal in dignity. One commentary of Genesis points out the significance of the creation of Eve from Adam: "She was not made out of his head to surpass him, nor from his feet to be trampled on, but from his side to

be equal to him, and near his heart to be dear to him"
(Jamieson, Fausset and Brown, Commentary On The Whole
Bible). What a way to put it! This is what we were originally
made for – **to be equal in dignity but different in nature to
man** and to be cherished as a beautiful creature of God. In
fact, Saint John Paul the Great, referred to women as 'the
crown of creation', which also makes sense because the line of
creation in Genesis only gets more beautiful and complicated
and ultimately ends with us! This is not to say that women are
better than men or vice-versa, but it serves to highlight and
celebrate our differences. So when we're not being treated with
equal dignity and not being respected and cherished by those
around us, especially by the men in our lives, we instinctively
feel that something is not right. Eve felt this after the Original
Fall, as lust and other sins invaded her relationship with Adam.
All women, except Mary, have suffered from the same
consequences of sin since.

But there is good news! And that is that we have been
redeemed by Jesus! He continually encourages us to start anew,
to go back to the beginning and He promises us to be with us
every step of the way:

"So if anyone is in Christ, there is a new
creation: everything old has passed away;
see, everything has become new!"
(2 Corinthians 5:17).

We are called to embrace God's original plan for us, to
embrace our femininity and dignity and to see ourselves and

others the way He sees us – worthy of love, care and respect, and beautiful both inside and out. If women are given a special kind of beauty as the 'crown of creation', with it comes a special kind of responsibility. But what is true beauty? And what do we do with it? Or better yet, what does God want us to do with any of the gifts He has given us? Basically, He wants us to rejoice in them and use them in the building of His kingdom, and we're now going to try to unpack what this means for us women.

Being Original

So by now we have established three important facts:

1.   God has created us in His image and likeness, and He said it was **'very good'**.

2.   God has created us all **equal in dignity** but different in nature (man and woman) and we are all worthy of love and respect.

3.   Women were given **beauty as a special gift** which means we as women also have a special responsibility.

We know we were made in God's image and likeness which sounds great, but this fact becomes even more amazing when we know who God is. We may think this is impossible to know, I mean, it's GOD, right? Wrong. Being the wonderful Father He is, He decided to let us know and He uncovers

Himself through the Scriptures. We read that God is our Refuge, our Fortress, our Strength; He is gracious, righteous, full of compassion, mighty, awesome, beautiful. He's our everything (just read the Psalms)! But what always would strike me the most was this: God is love (1 John 4:16). **He creates us out of love, in love, for love and to love.** A lot of love right there. To be original then, in the way God planned for us, means reflecting this love. We do this through the way we act and speak around others and ourselves. Furthermore, to show His love towards His daughters, He gave us women a special gift of beauty, through which we can reflect His beauty and glory.

Original Beauty

Now, maybe you don't feel beautiful, maybe you think you need to be a certain size or look like those women in the magazines and on TV to be beautiful. This is what our culture tells us we should look like to be beautiful, happy and wanted. But looking like a supermodel is not what true beauty is about. The world tells us that we need to be tall, but not too tall, skinny but not too skinny, with this kind of hair and those kind of eyes...aaaaahhh! It can be exhausting living up to all those standards! But luckily, we don't have to. As followers of Christ, we don't look to our culture's standards, but to God's standards for everything, including beauty. God defines beauty because He created it. Beauty flows from Him because He Himself is beautiful (Isaiah 33:17; Psalm 26:4 [27:4]).

So we've established that beauty is a gift, including physical beauty. Our bodies are a gift and are certainly not bad nor dirty. In fact, they are very good because God created them – therefore, physical beauty is also very good. But physical beauty can become very bad when it doesn't flow from internal beauty – the beauty of your soul.

I want you to stop and think about the religious sisters or the godly women you have met during your lifetime. I bet you would say they were beautiful. That is because women of God radiate a joy, beauty and purity that comes from having a heart firmly placed in God's hands. Therefore, it is fair to say that we are beautiful, both inside and out, when our hearts and lives are in accordance with God's plan for us. This is when we act, speak and dress as daughters of a King, remembering His love for us and our vocation to show this love to others through the gifts we have been given.

Looking to our Older Sisters

So how are we to behave, speak and dress? Scriptures are full of godly women, our sisters in Christ and we can learn a lot from them, especially from Mary. However, one of my favourite 'guidelines' has to be Proverbs 31. Proverbs 31 is a story of a woman of God– she's hardworking, kind, modest, charitable, wise, strong, fearless, happy and, most importantly, focused on the Lord. It's a tall order – she sounds perfect – but Proverbs 31 is not about perfection. It's about perseverance in the path to holiness and faithfulness to God. This is all God wants from us as women. If we were then to talk to our Proverbs 31 woman for advice, what would she say?

1.   **How should we behave?** Work on being kind, trustworthy, gracious, patient, discerning and hardworking. You may not be buying a field like she is, but you will make big decisions in your lifetime where you'll need to discern carefully. You may not be afraid of snowfall, but you still have fears you will need to face. You may not be making linen garments, bed coverings or clothes, but you still have daily tasks that you are called to complete. Holiness does not consist only of being on your knees and praying. It also consists of doing! Many saints knew this and often cautioned against idleness because 'it teaches us all kind of vice' (St John Bosco). We should be working hard and with passion at the tasks in front of us, whether this is schoolwork, housework or extra-curricular activities. Having said that, we should also know how to laugh, rejoice and rest as God instructed us to do.

2.   **How should we speak?** Our Proverbs 31 woman "opens her mouth with wisdom, and the teaching of kindness is on her tongue" (Proverbs 31:26). We women often have a way with words and we can sometimes have sharp tongues that hurt friends and loved ones. Not only that, but vulgar and impure conversations, which are so prevalent in the media and culture, hurt not only those who are listening but also the one doing the talking. Let us therefore think about

the consequences of our words and make sure that what we say builds up and encourages those around us (Ephesians 4:29).

3. **How should we dress?** Neither the Bible nor the Catholic Church have a set of rules for how we should dress. Deep down we know which kind of clothes only reveal our body and which reveal our true beauty and dignity as women. Our bodies and souls are intimately connected. We all want to be noticed, known, acknowledged and loved for who we truly are, but the truth is that when we reveal more of our bodies, we are not revealing more of who we are but less. This means we are using our beauty in the wrong way and paving the way for impurity of soul and mind in both us and our brothers and sisters. By dressing immodestly, we are inviting everyone, and especially our brothers in Christ, to focus on our bodies instead of our souls. Deep down we know that this is not true love. So we turn to our Proverbs 31 woman for inspiration: "Strength and dignity are her clothing, and she laughs at the time to come" (Proverbs 31:25). This is obviously a modest but stylish woman! Because she is aware of her strength and dignity as a woman, it reflects not only in her clothing but in her behaviour. She trusts our Lord so completely that she can laugh at the time to come! Modest clothing doesn't mean frumpy-sack-of-potatoes-no-colour clothing. Modesty in clothing, as well as in speech and behaviour, is an invitation to find your own style that reflects who you really are instead of revealing what the culture wants

you to be – just a body.

I hope I've managed to communicate the awesomeness of being a woman. I remember the first time I heard the good news about who I am as a woman, what God had planned for me from the beginning and what a beautiful gift womanhood is – it sounded amazing but slightly unbelievable and unattainable. Maybe it sounds like that to you. It may take a while to sink in because our minds have been stuffed with messages claiming the opposite of what you just read, but I encourage you to be patient and pray that God helps you along the way. Understanding who we are and acting accordingly actually invites and gives freedom to others around you to do the same. Venerable Fulton Sheen perhaps put it best when he said:

> "To a great extent the level of any civilization is the level of its womanhood. When a man loves a woman, he has to become worthy of her. The higher her virtue, the more her character, the more devoted she is to truth, justice, goodness, the more a man has to aspire to be worthy of her. The history of civilization could actually be written in terms of the level of its women."

Wow! What a beautiful invitation for us women to grow in virtue. And in accepting this invitation, we change the world for the better and teach others to do the same! We truly become the 'salt of the earth' and 'light of the world' (Matthew

5:13-16).

God's Plan for Our Sexuality

A lot of what we've mentioned so far sets the foundation for our life as women who want to live chastely. Focused on God and what He is calling us to do and be, we can adjust our lives to what God is and wants us to be – free, loved, joyful, beautiful and pure. This is what being original means and this is what chastity is all about.

Our culture tells us that chastity and purity are just about a series of silly restrictions that say that sexuality is bad and dirty. But this couldn't be further from the truth that our Church teaches! We have already established that our bodies are a gift from God, and so is sexuality. It is a gift, however, that He intended for marriage as a blessing through which two become one flesh (Ephesians 5:31). The Church believes our sexuality is so beautiful and sacred that it can bring two bodies and souls into one. In fact, the relationship between husband and wife is so sacred that it is compared to the relationship between Christ and His bride – the Church (Ephesians 5:32). This gives such a profound dimension to our sexuality - one which should not be so treated so lightly nor easily discarded as our culture tells us.

I heard a priest once explain that chastity is not one big NO – it's a lot of little NOs that lead to one big and awesome

YES. When we respect our sexual desires and urges, but still understand that they are gift from God that we can transform into a pure and selfless gift for our spouses in marriage, we are saying one big YES to true and authentic love and God's plan for love between man and woman.

We're all afraid of being alone and not chosen so we're tempted to settle for less instead of God's amazing plans for our lives. But you have already been chosen, you are never alone and you are always loved, and have been since the day you were conceived. You were made for authentic and true love, so reach for it!

Chastity, however, is not just about purity of the body but also purity of the heart, mind and soul – emotional chastity. Our emotions and passions are also a gift from God but, just like with all our other gifts after the Fall of Man, they can be used to deceive us and those around us instead of revealing the truth about others and our relationships. Sarah Swafford puts it this way: "Emotional Virtue, then, is the right ordering of our thoughts, actions, and desires as they relate to our relationships" (www.emotionalvirtue.com). It means guarding our hearts and not letting our emotions and passions run wild and free (Proverbs 4:32). It means taking care of our hearts and minds but also the hearts and minds of others.

We women should be especially careful here. It happens so often – incessant daydreaming about a boy we just met, a romantic comedy or book that leaves us with unrealistic expectations and fantasies for days, using a male friend emotionally so we feel desired and loved (friend-zoning). Does this mean that we should stay away from male friends, lock ourselves up in a dark room with no media entertainment whatsoever? No. But it does mean that we should constantly be discerning our thoughts and emotions and making sure that what we are doing, watching, reading and listening to is directed towards truth, love and goodness. In practice it also means that we should be looking at our brothers in Christ primarily as brothers and not instantly as boyfriend or husband material – we should rejoice in their personalities, gifts and talents instead of using them emotionally as objects for our own purposes.

It is important to know boundaries in our relationships with others. These boundaries are more easily set when we realize the dignity and worth of each man and woman. When we recognize these boundaries in purity of heart, mind and body, we are then truly free daughters of God. We as women have a deep yearning to be loved and to love the way God loves us - completely, totally and endlessly - so let us keep that in mind in our relationships with others.

Living in Purity

Remembering everything you now know about who you are and God's plans for as a woman, here are a few steps you can take on your journey as a daughter of God:

1.   Pray and Read

You probably hear this all the time, but prayer truly is the most powerful weapon we have in spiritual battle and the greatest comfort in everyday life. Prayer is simply having a conversation with your greatest friend and loving Father – the One who understands you completely, sees everything that goes on in your life, wants what is best for you and wants to help you! The Almighty Creator just wants you to be truly happy and holy. So pray. And more importantly, pray regularly. The Catholic tradition of prayer and the Scriptures are so beautifully rich that we really have no excuse not to pray. Do some research, take a while to discover different types of prayer and see which one works best for you at this present moment (check out Chapters 3 and 4). You might want to try praying with Scripture, the liturgy of the hours, a novena or the rosary. Whatever you choose, do it regularly. And don't be afraid to switch it up every now and then. Just keep a steady line of communication with your Father!

Having said that, relationships go both ways. You may have a lot to share with our Heavenly Father, but He also has a lot to tell you – and He has said it all through the Scriptures. Feeling sad? Need encouragement or just a reminder of God's love and glory? Looking for advice? It's all there in the Scriptures, you just need to read it.

Quick tip: Saying a prayer or reading a passage from the Bible in the morning as soon as you wake up might make you more mindful of His presence during the day. By doing the same at night, while looking over the day with all its successes and mistakes, He may point out some

things you can work on or simply rejoice
with you over the good things that
happened that day.

2.   Look to Mary

Having said all that about prayer, I highly recommend you regularly pray the Rosary. Why? Because a sure way to get to Jesus is through His mother Mary. Not only is she Jesus' mother, she is also our mother. She waits to hear from you and takes all that you tell her straight to her Son. Also, she's a woman. A perfect one at that. She knows all the ins and outs of being a woman and wants nothing more than to teach you how to be a true woman of God.

I was once advised to talk to Mary as I would to my earthly mother, respectfully but still as her child. I share about my day, I moan, I complain, I cry and laugh when talking to my own earthly mother, and you bet I try to do the same with Mary. She's endlessly kind, gentle, courageous and patient – everything I want to be – so she can definitely deal with the truck-load of problems we set at her feet.

Quick tip: Read about Mary in the Scriptures and pay attention to what she says and does. Try to imitate some of her virtues and ask for her intercession.

3.   Regularly Participate in the Sacraments

Our God wants to be close to us. We're His children and Scripture repeats on multiple occasions that He longs for us. In fact, we can take the whole Bible as a love story between God and His people. He came down from heaven to be with us in human flesh with all its struggles and continues to do so in the Holy Eucharist. He loves us that much!

"For God so loved the world that he gave his only Son, so that everyone who believes in him may not perish but may have eternal life" (John 3:16).

When we eat His flesh and drink His blood, He changes us – He cleans our hearts and souls, restores us and gives us eternal life. Therefore, I cannot emphasize enough how important it is to attend Holy Mass every Sunday (check out Chapter 6). St John Vianney once said that if we truly understood the Mass, we would die from joy! We may not always feel excited about Holy Mass, but Mass is not primarily about us. It's about Him – and He's always excited and happy to see us! We may not understand the Mass completely, but we can try to read about it and ask God to teach us. We may even want to spend some time in Adoration just praying in front of the Blessed Sacrament. He waits for us there every Sunday in the Flesh, and the graces that flow from His presence are amazingly great even if we don't see them.

To be able to fully receive these graces, going to confession is a must. We may fall into all kinds of sins, we may feel burdened and broken, and beyond repair, but there is no evil God hasn't already conquered, no wound He hasn't or wouldn't heal. He invites us:

> "Come to me, all you that are weary and are carrying heavy burdens, and I will give you rest" (Matthew 11:28).

The Sacrament of Reconciliation is God's way of releasing you from the snares of sin and healing your wounds, and He does that through his servant, the priest in the Sacrament. Truly it is a fresh start, and because His mercy is endless, He waits patiently for us every time we sin. Be not afraid - just go.

I love this quote by Edith Stein. She was an awesome woman of God and she understood how important and liberating participation in the life of the Church is:

> "Participation in the divine life has a liberating power in itself; it lessens the weight of our earthly concerns and grants us a bit of eternity even in this finitude, a reflection of beatitude, a transformation into light. But the invitation to this transformation in God's land is given to us by God Himself in the liturgy of the Church. Therefore the life of an authentic

Catholic woman is also a liturgical life.
Whoever prays together with the Church
in spirit and in truth knows that her whole
life must be formed by this life of prayer."

Let us all be authentic Catholic woman and turn to our God in the sacraments.

Quick tip: Attending daily Mass
throughout the week when you can, and
spending time in Adoration are great ways
to further develop your relationship with
God.

4.   Find Support and Be Support

It can be hard living according to God's Word in a world that lives so differently. We can start doubting our decision to be true women of God and convince ourselves that this or that sin really isn't that bad. This has happened to me and through it I have learned to cling ever more tightly to God's Word and the Sacraments, but I have also come to understand that we humans, especially women, are relational beings. Having a friend who understands, supports and keeps me accountable and focused is a blessing and gift from God Himself because He understands my need for it. So try to surround yourself with people who have the same goal as you – to be holy and go to our heavenly home, and try to help and encourage those around you who are dealing with the same struggles you have had.

Quick tip: Youth groups, retreats and pilgrimages are great places to meet new friends, develop godly friendships and learn more about your faith.

Some final thoughts…

A woman's love is meant to be fruitful - not only physically but spiritually. Through loving and receiving others into our hearts we give life to them – and this life and love only spreads! How awesome is that!

Once you encounter and receive the living God, you will not be able to keep it to yourself – because in receiving His love you receive true life, and a woman wants nothing more but to give life and love to others. Have you ever listened to a woman in love? She cannot stop talking about it and sharing her joy with others. This is not a weakness as the world may tell you! By loving we receive love. Our faith is truly paradoxical in that sense – the more you sincerely give, the more you will receive (Luke 6:38). So do not be afraid of loving and being loved, especially in your relationship with God. He loves us more than anyone else and wants only the very best for us. Better still, because He made us, He knows exactly what will make us feel truly happy and fulfilled – so trust Him!

I'd like to end with this quote from Pope Emeritus Benedict XVI. It serves as a great reminder that when we live our lives the way God meant it, embracing our womanhood, its vocation and gifts, we lose nothing but gain all:

> "If we let Christ into our lives, we lose nothing, nothing, absolutely nothing of what makes life free, beautiful and great... I say to you, dear young people: Do not be afraid of Christ! He takes nothing away, and He gives you everything. When we give ourselves to Him, we receive a hundredfold in return. Yes, open, open wide the doors to Christ — and you will find true life."

Want to know more?

Books:

- Theology of the Body for Beginners (Christopher West)
- Theology of Her Body (Crystalina Evert)
- Emotional Virtue: A Guide to Drama-Free Relationships (Sarah Swafford)
- Pure Womanhood (Crystalina Evert)

Websites:

- Chastity Project
- The Catholic Young Woman
- Life Teen Blog
- Focus Blog

CHAPTER 9: THEOLOGY OF THE BODY FOR HIM
Matt Corrigan

Matt Corrigan is a full-time missionary and youth worker as part of the Sion Community. He is a gifted napper, loves American football, libraries and wishes life was more like a musical. He's passionate about encouraging all people to be the person God created them to be.

There are a lot of voices in our culture telling us what a man is and who we should be as men. But have you ever considered who you're called to be as a *man of God*? We live in a world where everything we want can be attained with a few clicks, and this isn't good for shaping us as men. It tells us that everything comes easy in life, but like my father taught me, nothing that's actually worth anything in life comes without a price.

It can be very confusing for us to live in this fast-paced, everything-right-now culture because we can make choices and get in over our head with things that aren't healthy for us. But in "the beginning it was not so" (Matthew 19:8). God created us for good, He gives us desires and dreams that are to help us find our way in life and ultimately to show us the path towards Him, who can do infinitely more than we can ask or imagine (Ephesians 3:20), we just have to be willing to let Him. This might sound scary, living a life contrary to what the world tells you will make you happy might sound daunting, but Pope Francis offers us some encouragement: 'Pay attention, my

169

young friends: to go against the current; this is good for the heart, but we need courage to swim against the tide.' We need to swim against the tide, for our sake and for the sake of others, and we need to move forward with hope towards our God. As Pope St John Paul II, the patron saint of young people and the man who gave us the Theology of the Body told us: 'Be not afraid'. We are called to make a stand, to stand up for Jesus and let His gaze of love sustain us, and to encourage others to do the same.

Men are created in the image and likeness of God (Genesis 1:26). Within each of us is the capability to show the strength, integrity, courage and protective nature of God to the world. This isn't something only available to a select group of men, but something that is in all men. To explore and discover who God is calling us to be as men after His own heart (1 Samuel 13:14) we shall look at what it means, firstly, to be a son of God, then a brother to our fellow brothers, and finally to be a brother to our sisters in Christ.

Who are we as sons of God?

"For all who are led by the Spirit of God are children of God. For you did not receive a spirit of slavery to fall back into fear, but you have received a spirit of adoption. When we cry, 'Abba! Father!' it is that very Spirit bearing witness with our spirit that we are children of God" (Romans 8:14-16).

Before we can look at who God might be calling us to be in the future, or what He even expects of us in the here and now, we must first recognise who we are, and more importantly who the Lord says we are. In doing so we will start to learn more about ourselves and our gifts, talents and uniqueness in His eyes, and eventually we discover not only *who* we are, but we proclaim to the world *whose* we are.

Led by the Spirit

The passage above from Romans tells us that all who are led by the Spirit are sons of God. In that sense everyone is a child of God, and of course we all have that possibility. But what does it mean to be led by the Spirit?

The Holy Spirit is the love between the Father and the Son. The One who empowers us to be all that we can be and gives us special gifts. Being led by Him is more of a matter of us allowing Him to decide what is best for us in our lives, rather than relying on our own abilities and decision making skills. It means that we must give up control and allow our heavenly Father to direct us. It is in accepting that our Father knows what is best for us and turning away from all the things in life that would hold us back that we ultimately find freedom and fulfilment. The author of The Chronicles of Narnia, C.S. Lewis, put it this way in his book 'Mere Christianity':

> 'The more we let God take us over, the
> more truly ourselves we become – because
> He made us. He invented us. He invented
> all the different people that you and I were
> intended to be...It is when I turn to Christ,
> when I give up myself to His personality,
> that I first begin to have a real personality
> of my own.'

What is left for us, after giving ourselves up to the Father, is to then follow. It is up to us to commit ourselves to him and to the way He calls us to live our lives. At its heart, to be led by the Spirit is to follow.

Sons not slaves

We hopefully know by now that we are sons of God. Sons of the Most High King, no less. St Paul in Romans tells us so, and that we are called out of slavery. But what have we been, and can we be, enslaved to? Our sin.

God our Father loves us, we must know this first. It is because He loves us so much that He sent His only Son to die for our sins (John 3:16). But it is also because He loves us so much that He calls us to more. We need to take our sin seriously, with the knowledge that we are loved, but still called to put sin behind us. If we are to follow God's plan for us as men, we need to take a serious look at ourselves and decide if the life we are living is really fitting for a son of God. St Paul tells us in Ephesians about renouncing our sin:

"But fornication and impurity of any kind,
or greed, must not even be mentioned
among you, as is proper among
saints. Entirely out of place is obscene,
silly, and vulgar talk; but instead, let there
be thanksgiving. Be sure of this, that no
fornicator or impure person, or one who is
greedy (that is, an idolater), has any
inheritance in the kingdom
of Christ and of God.
Let no one deceive you with empty words,
for because of these things the wrath of
God comes on those who are
disobedient. Therefore do not be
associated with them. For once you were
darkness, but now in the Lord you are
light. Live as children of light"
(Ephesians 5:3-8)

As men we are called to purity. Purity of thought, of heart and in our actions. We are called to love others, and not to use them for the satisfaction of our own desires. Whilst many would tell you that pornography, masturbation and other sexual sin is harmless and only natural, our Father warns us against it because He knows what is best for us. We are to be *sons and not slaves*. These kinds of things aren't healthy or good for us, and are certainly not harmless. This isn't said to make us feel guilty, but so that we know that there is so much more: real, pure, true, authentic love exists, is attainable, and is worth it. God wants us to experience it, and so if and when you struggle with these sorts of temptations, remember two things: God loves you, and you are not alone in fighting the battle. You have brothers fighting the same battle alongside you (more on that later!).

You owe it to yourself to keep persevering and fighting. Two ways you can do this are through prayer and the Sacrament of Reconciliation. Praying to God for purity is a way to help sustain yourself in the fight, whilst the Sacrament of Reconciliation shows us His love and mercy when we acknowledge our mistakes. Here the Son of God sets us free, and who the Son sets free is free indeed (John 8:36).

Don't fear the Sacrament! Pope Francis says that going to the Sacrament of Reconciliation isn't meant to be like going to a torture chamber, but we should see it as a place to get right with God. He's waiting to forgive you and give you the grace to carry on. Keep persevering in the battle against temptation, it's worth it, and victory is certainly possible through the strength that Christ gives us. *Remember, you are a son, not a slave.*

We cry Abba! Father!

Our God is a good Father. He is constantly wanting to pour out His love on us. Like the father of the prodigal son (Luke 15:20), he is always waiting patiently for us to turn back to him, to cry 'Abba! Father!' No matter how long it takes, He waits for us, and He knows how to give good gifts to His children. He is the one we can always rely on. Through His

Son, Jesus, He has already won the victory on the cross for us. We have to open ourselves to receive His love.

"Ask, and it will be given you; search, and you will find; knock, and the door will be opened for you. For everyone who asks receives, and everyone who searches finds, and for everyone who knocks, the door will be opened. Is there anyone among you who, if your child asks for bread, will give a stone? Or if the child asks for a fish, will give a snake? If you then, who are evil, know how to give good gifts to your children, how much more will your Father in heaven give good things to those who ask him!" (Matthew 7:7-11).

We must learn to trust Him. We must know that God is there guiding us, and that He wants what is best for us. In practice, living life as a son of the Father means choosing not to believe the lies of the world that tell you 'you aren't good enough' or 'you aren't worthy of God's love.' The truth is we can never make ourselves worthy or good enough, but that doesn't stop Him loving us anyway. ***Try it:*** today, right now, say to God:

God, my Father,

I choose to believe in who you say I am.

I reject the lies that would tell me I'm
unworthy of Your love,

and I live today in the knowledge that I am
a son of Yours. And if a son, then an heir,

an heir to Your kingdom.
(cf. Romans 8:17)

Do not be afraid to call upon God your Father, who is ever ready to support, guide and strengthen you on your journey of faith.

Who are we as brothers to one another?

'How very good and pleasant it is
when kindred live together in unity!'
(Psalm 122:1 [133:1])

Someone once told me: 'If you want to go fast, go alone. But if you want to go far, go together.' It's so true that in order for us to reach our potential as men we need people around us who recognise what is best for us and will do whatever it takes to call it out of us, and allow us to do the same for them. We need people who want to share the journey with us and will keep us accountable when we aren't being our best selves. We need to have other guys around us with the same good and healthy goals as us - pursuing their dreams, chasing after God and helping us to do the same.

Band of Brothers

There's no way that I would be the person I am without the encouragement, support, help and guidance of my brothers in Christ. I've been blessed with one real brother who loves and supports me. But there are also a number of other men of my age in my life who believe the same things as me, are striving for the same things in life as me, and ultimately are helping me on the path to holiness: **the path towards Jesus**.

Scripture tells us to encourage one another and use both our words and actions to build each other up. That can mean speaking up for a friend or simply standing by them when they are in need. I love the story of three young men called Shadrach, Meshach and Abednego, in the book of Daniel. These men stuck by their friend Daniel, and stood by each other in the face of death when Nebuchadnezzar, the king of Babylon, told them to deny their belief in God and bow before his golden idol. Each of them refused to bow to this statue, and would rather have been burned than give up on God (Daniel 3:18). That is true faithfulness, to God firstly, but also to each other.

Friendships like these take effort, intention and time. When we speak of such friends we're not merely talking of people who will show up on your birthday, or who you can hang out and watch the game with. It's not that there is anything wrong with either of those things, but we as men need to go deeper in our friendships. Think of the paralysed man who was carried by his friends through a roof to meet Jesus (Luke 5:18-20). They saw how their friend needed Jesus and would have done whatever it took to make sure he got there.

If you don't feel like you have friends like that, who will carry you towards Christ when you can't walk, who are willing to share both the adventures and the difficulties of life with you, then pray! Ask God to show you the kind of people He wants to be these good friends for you, and then seek them out yourself. It takes effort to make good and lasting friendships, but I can guarantee you'll find that it's worth it. Christ Himself is also our brother, and so we must not forget to welcome Him into our current friendships. It is when we do this that we can begin to share our lives more deeply with others.

Accountability

'Two are better than one...For if they fall, one will lift up the other' (Ecclesiastes 4:9-10).

What do I mean by sharing deeply with close friends? In short, it means that we share our dreams, our hopes and plans for the future, but also our shortcomings, worries and doubts.

When we do this we must do it in a spirit of openness and love, allowing our brothers to correct us when we need it and lovingly doing the same for them when the moment calls for it. As St Peter encourages us: "Now that you have purified your souls by your obedience to the truth so that you have genuine mutual love, love one another deeply from the heart" (1 Peter 1:22). When we keep each other accountable, we help purify ourselves and our brothers through obedience to the truth we share with each other, in love. Who we share with is also important. Make sure it is someone you trust and respect as a brother in Christ, someone who will challenge you to become the Saint whom God is calling you to become.

It will be hard at first, and will take time to build up trust to be open in sharing your personal struggles, but it will be of great benefit for you in the battle for purity and holiness. As I said earlier, we men are called to purity. This might initially sound like an old-fashioned or maybe even feminine quality, but men are called to share in it too. A man who seeks purity is a strong man, and we are called to demonstrate that strength to the world. But we should never forget that through Christ – the greatest Friend and Brother we have – we can do all things (Philippians 4:13), so always remember to turn to Christ in times of struggle and ask for His strength in you to say 'no' to the temptation and 'yes' to His grace.

At this point you might be wondering what the next step is once you're on board with the idea of a band of brothers. Sharing your life with them can make so much sense in theory, but how do you put it into practice? To offer you a rough practical guide, here's a brief model which has worked well for me and my brothers for how you could share your thoughts, emotions, highs and lows. See this as a starting point to trigger the thoughts and feelings that you want to share with your brothers or seek their advice over.

PRISE...

P- Physical: How am I feeling physically? Do I feel healthy or unwell in any way? Am I looking after myself well in terms of how much sleep I get, how much I'm exercising, and in what I eat?

R- Relational: How are my relationships with family, friends and the people I'm around? Is there anyone I particularly struggle with? How can I seek to resolve it? Is there anyone I either need to forgive, or apologise to?

I- Intellectual: How am I exercising my brain? Do I spend more time than is wise on computers, games consoles or watching TV? Am I coping with my school work? Do I feed my mind with good and healthy things?

S- Spiritual: Do I make enough time for God in my life? Am I receiving the Sacraments regularly enough? Do I put the will of God before other people's expectations of me?

E- Emotional: How am doing on the inside? Is there anything that's upsetting me, stressing me out, or that I'm struggling to deal with? Am I at peace within myself?

One final question you can ask is: Is there anything that I don't want to share?

This can be very difficult, but it could be the one thing that is holding you back! It takes courage to share these things, but that openness strengthens the bonds you have with your brothers.

Following this method with your own band of brothers can really help you in the battle of life. It's another weapon in your armoury that will help you stay strong. Keep on fighting, brothers!

Who are we as brothers to our sisters?

"Let mutual love continue"
(Hebrews 13:1).

At the beginning of this chapter we discussed how men, who are created in the image and likeness of God (Genesis 1:26), show to the world a part of who God is: His strength, leadership and total giving of Himself. But we have yet to speak of the ways in which women reveal the nature of God to us and how we are supposed to relate to them.

There's a reason men are so fascinated by women, and we desire relationship and intimacy (physically, emotionally and spiritually) with them. Women, too, are created in the image and likeness of God. They reflect the beauty, care and loving nature of Him. The scriptures are full of imagery about the beauty of women, and it's because of God that we're able to see that in them. Appreciating the beauty of women is good because it's part of God's original design! It's how we respond to that beauty that can either lead to us closer to Christ or lead us into sin.

My favourite book in the Old Testament, Tobit, tells the story of a young man called Tobias who is guided by the Archangel Raphael to take a young woman called Sarah as his wife. Raphael describes Sarah to him as 'sensible, brave, and very beautiful' (Tobit 6:12). It is in this way that the women in our lives show us the face of God. But it's something much more than just physical beauty that draws us to them – it's something deeply spiritual and emotional as well.

We have these desires towards women, including sexual desires, and because God put them in us they are good and healthy and normal. However, God also calls us to control and direct them properly, in order that we can love properly. As St JP2 said in 'Love and Responsibility': 'A person's rightful due is to be treated as an object of love, not as an object for use,' and so we must never put our own desires before the good of another, especially in this area.

So much damage has been done to women by men. Yes, they may have wounded us too. But we must earnestly seek the best for the women in our lives, to love them 'as Christ loved the church and gave himself up for her' (Ephesians 5:25). In my own life I think of my mother and sister, I would do whatever it takes to uphold their dignity and self-worth, and to show them the love of Christ. It is our responsibility as men to do this for **all** the women in our lives – mothers, sisters, friends, girlfriends and, if God calls us to marriage, our wives. Again as the great St JP2 once said: 'It is the duty of every man to uphold the dignity of every woman.' The way we do this is always to seek to honour them.

Honour thy mother and father (and sisters!)

"outdo one another in showing honour"
(Romans 12:10).

Our words and actions have both great and terrible power. What we do and say can 'destroy' and 'build' (Jeremiah 1:9-10). So, when considering the women in our lives, we need to ensure that we treat them with respect and never as an object for use. Sadly, the culture we live in tries to overthrow this idea. It tells us we should indulge our desires and lusts. It tells us that to do so is inherently masculine. This couldn't be further from the truth. Ask yourself: what takes greater strength? To indulge our sexual urges, whether that be through sex or pornography, or to say no to that in the hope of greater things to come – authentic, true love? In saying 'no' to the wrong things now, we are saying 'yes' to the right things in the future.

But God isn't just asking us to repress these desires until marriage so that we can indulge them then. He asks us to *transform* them now so that we can participate in the purity of true love, prepare to offer ourselves as a gift in marriage or priesthood, and for the even greater glory we will encounter in heaven. We can commit to honouring our sisters now, in the present moment, by choosing what's best for them in every situation, by encouraging and praying for them in their highs and lows in life. In doing so we prepare ourselves and them for whatever God has for us in the future.

By choosing what's best for the women in our lives, we're also choosing what's best for the wife and family God may grant us in the future. By endeavouring to grow in self-control, selflessness and respect, we become more able to effectively lead, love, protect and provide for our family in the way God asks us to. Also, by living a pure lifestyle now we reinforce the God-given worth we see in our future wife by proving we're willing to wait for her.

Boundaries

In order to demonstrate this level of respect towards women and our commitment to defending their dignity, we must maintain appropriate boundaries between ourselves and our sisters in Christ. That might sound restrictive, and you may be expecting a list of do's and don'ts, but don't be put off. There is actually great freedom in boundaries!

Boundaries are essential in making our intentions clear at all times, building trust and ensuring that both we and the women around us are secure in our relationships. When we talk about boundaries between us and women, the first thing we must always remember is that good, strong boundaries stem from the heart. If our heart is in the right place, then we will be seeking to act first and foremost from a place of honour. Primarily towards God, then to our sisters, but also to ourselves. If the attitude of your heart is right then your actions will follow. This may not necessarily all fall into place at once, easily or comfortably, but Jesus didn't come to make us comfortable, He came to call us to greatness. Aiming to purify our hearts and refine our actions in order to uphold the natural worth of every woman puts us firmly on that route to greatness.

> "Or do you not know that your body is a temple of the Holy Spirit within you...? For you were bought with a price; therefore glorify God in your body"
> (1 Corinthians 6:19-20)

We should remember that our body and the bodies of those around us are sacred. Every person has been bought at the great price of Jesus' death, even if they don't believe it or know it, and so we should treat them accordingly. Our bodies are temples of the Holy Spirit, so we should likewise respect ourselves. In terms of boundaries, this means that we should not only make sure we don't push physical boundaries, but go even further by trying to avoid putting ourselves in positions where we may be tempted to do so.

I don't want to go into a list of rules about 'how far is too far', because I think if we're honest with ourselves then most of us know when our physical behaviour towards women is crossing a line that it shouldn't. If you're seeking to to honour your sisters, then one of the first things you'll naturally recognise is the need to avoid pushing their boundaries, because then we can carry out our duty to help them in their fight for purity as well.

In a healthy relationship, if you really love the girl you're with then you will put her journey with God, her purity, and protecting her heart above your own desires. This can mean doing things you don't want to do (or not doing the things you want to do), which might sound hard, but true love always involves sacrifice – as Jesus showed us when He demonstrated His love for us by giving up His life (John 15:13).

If you're not in a relationship, it's still just as important to guard the hearts of the women around you. When we give mixed messages it's not only confusing but also unfair: those cheeky nudges might seem harmless to you, but they can lead women into thinking you're interested in more. Whether you are or you aren't interested in pursuing her romantically, you owe it to her to be clear on what the relationship means to you, to protect both of you from avoidable heartbreak.

Alongside physical boundaries, it's equally important for us to be aware of emotional boundaries. We need to have wisdom in what we share with our sisters about ourselves – we can't jump into sharing deep parts of our lives with someone we haven't known very long, because our relationship with them may not be able to handle it. It takes time to build mutual trust based on solid friendships, wherever the relationship may be headed in future.

However scary or restricting this might sound right now, always remember:

1) Boundaries are above all an attitude of the heart.

2) You were bought at a price, which means you deserve respect and have a duty to give it.

3) You can *choose* to claim the freedom of boundaries.

Jesus died to show us how much we're really worth, so we should live in a way that proclaims our worth. It's worth it!

Some final thoughts...

Having read all this, you may be thinking that you could never live up to all that we are called to, and perhaps you feel like you're not 'man enough'. If so, you are not alone! The key is not to listen to the voice inside you that tells us that, because it's not the truth, and it's not from God. Remember those words we heard earlier from JP2: **'be not afraid'**. No matter how many times you may have failed in this area, no matter how many times you continue to fall, never stop picking yourself up and returning to Jesus: He is waiting for you. Continue to "run with perseverance the race that is set out" before you (Hebrews 12:1). He isn't unrealistic, He doesn't expect perfection overnight – all He asks is that you are *striving* for holiness, and that you continue to make the effort. God will give you His strength.

> "ask him that your ways may be made straight and that all your paths and plans may prosper"
> (Tobit 3:19).

Jesus doesn't promise that it will be easy, but He does promise that it will be worth it. In Matthew 7, He says:

> "Enter through the narrow gate; for the gate is wide and the road is easy that leads to destruction, and there are many who take it. For the gate is narrow and the road is hard that leads to life, and there are few who find it" (Matthew 7:13-14).

Seek the narrow gate. If you continue to seek God's will for your life in this way, He will show you the path to fulfilment in this life and His glory in the next. You have what it takes. **Trust Him.**

Want to know more?

Books:

- Theology of the Body for Beginners (Christopher West)
- Theology of His Body (Jason Evert)
- Wild at Heart (John Eldredge)
- Killing Lions (Sam Eldredge)

Websites:

- And Sons Magazine
- Chastity Project
- The Catholic Gentlemen
- The Culture Project

CHAPTER 10: GOD'S MASTERPIECE – IDENTITY
Irene Chia

Irene is a full-time missionary passionate about bringing meaningful difference to lives she encounters. She loves being the voice for the unborn and encouraging people to their full potential. At any time if you are looking for her, just follow the trail of laughter or singing.

The Original Design

Magazines are filled with advertisements of products that showcase their beauty and the benefits they have for us, the viewers. It is fascinating to see the beauty they present and sometimes we are led to want to own those products, most especially when they come with a big name. Most of us like designer's goods because of the reputation they carry. A pair of Jimmy Choo shoes would definitely boost our confidence as we wear them. A man wearing an Armani suit would carry an aura of attraction with him. There is something about designer's goods that attracts us naturally. Some of the attributes would be the originality of the product, its uniqueness and the quality of it. We all love things that are original, unique and of high quality. And the greatest Designer's product of all is us, who are created in the image and likeness of the One True King. If we take a closer look at our lives, we will realise that we are not only a Designer's

Product but in fact we are a **masterpiece** of the **Divine Designer**.

Our Heavenly Father, who is the coolest designer of all, has from eternity called us His masterpiece. Masterpiece sounds huge, and in fact it is majestic. Merriam-Webster dictionary has fully defined masterpiece as;

1. a work done with extraordinary skill; especially: a supreme intellectual or artistic achievement

2. a piece of work presented to a medieval guild as evidence of qualification for the rank of master

We can clearly see that only a highly skilled master can produce a masterpiece and that is what we are in the eyes of the Creator because we are **original**, **unique** and of **high quality**. The proof of this is from the very Word spoken to us from God through the Bible. From His Word we know that we are fearfully and wonderfully made (Psalm 138:14 [139:14]), He knew us before we were conceived (Jeremiah 1:5) and He knit us together in our mother's womb (Psalm 138:13 [139:13]). Every part of our being is willed by our Creator God who is very interested in us.

From the beginning, our Good God has willed a Good

Plan for His Good Creation. When He created the world, one consistent message that He kept repeating was; "It is **good**" and when He accomplished creation on the sixth day with the climax of creating humankind in His image and likeness, He exclaimed "It is **very good**". What could possibly give such satisfaction to God? I can imagine His happy smiling face as He finished His work of creation, He must have looked really satisfied. I believe anyone of us would be the same. Imagine yourself working on an important project, a project that has a great connection to something you like. When you have finally accomplished project, how would you feel? I believe you would feel satisfied, grateful and have a sense of achievement. That would probably be God's feeling too.

Picture this: on the sixth day of Creation when God had in His mind to create Adam and Eve, He stopped for awhile. He took out His best mirror and said; "Let us make humankind in our image, according to our likeness" (Genesis 1:26). What could possibly be in the mind of God when He said that? I would imagine a great amount of goodness and hope in His creation of humankind. To know more about that would be a great adventure of going back to His original design; deep into the heart of our Abba Father. And that my dear friend is the calling and the purpose of our life.

From the Word of God, we know that each of us is created with a purpose and our life is willed by our Creator. **Our very life is a miracle.** And yet we happened! How wonderful it is to know that our lives are truly willed by our Heavenly Father. Our lives are not a coincidence but rather a result of the great love of God who has chosen us before the foundation of the world. We are truly loved into being. If God ceases to think about us, we would cease to exist. If He has willed our being, then He must have a purpose for us. If God has a purpose for our life, then we are called to find out what that purpose may be. After all, He called me a **masterpiece**, one crafted out of love. Logically, our lives should be looking really awesome. It is the delight of the Master to see His Masterpiece fulfilling the purpose to which it is called.

Let us now consider these questions;

- Do I treat myself as a **masterpiece**?

- Do I treat my neighbours as **masterpieces**?

Being really honest with myself, my answer to both the questions would have been no. I could not see myself as a masterpiece. In my teenage years, I was the popular kid in school. My grades were amazing, I was loud and opinionated. My academic achievements had gained me a lot of friends, though not all were sincere. Although I had a lot of so called 'followers', I was never really happy inside. I was not satisfied with the way I looked, I wished I have a better body figure, I wished my family was richer materially, I wished I could achieve perfection in my studies and in all these lies an inferior complex grew within me. I was searching for myself in places that told me lies. I tried to find my security in achievements, relationships and everything material. I didn't know Christ in a personal way. I was looking for acceptance and allowed myself to be led by the world's standard.

Many of us in one way or another can relate to this, as we start searching for ourselves in our adolescent years. The challenges are real and sometimes we feel like nobody understands us, most especially our parents. Therefore we start reaching out to our friends and sometimes we may mix with the wrong group. As Jim Rohn popularly quoted; "You are the average of the five persons you spent time with". I have realised how true this statement in my life is. Looking back at the time of my life when I would hang out with a group of drunkards and smokers, without realising it, I became one of them; spending my weekend drinking at the clubs.

But one season of my life was spent with a group of people - loving Christians, and that has changed me tremendously. That was also the season I decided to accept Jesus Christ as my only Lord and Saviour. My life has never been the same ever since then. When I fall in love with **Love**, I start to fall in love with me – the original me that was created in the image and likeness of God. I started to live as the masterpiece of the Divine Designer. So dear friends, it is important to consider what kind of friends we are spending our time with. If we spend time with God-loving people, we will learn about loving ourselves and our neighbour as ourselves. If our friends are a group of people who tease us negatively, we will find ourselves unable to progress. I encourage you to take a good look at your friendships and make a decision about what kind of life you desire.

Identity in Christ

Deep in our design, we all desire to be happy. Everyone loves to be around joyful people. Joy attracts and that joy is possible with Jesus Christ. When our first parents, Adam and Eve fell into sin in the Garden of Eden, we lost the friendship of God. The loss of communion with God has brought about despair to humankind; happiness becomes somewhat unnatural, providence becomes somewhat doubtful and we start to live in our own strength. We were no longer able to see ourselves as Masterpieces but we doubt our original goodness. But God in His infinite love and mercy made a plan to reconcile us to Him again.

"For God so loved the world that he gave
his only Son, so that everyone who
believes in him may not perish but may
have eternal life" (John 3:16).

When Jesus came to the world as a helpless baby, God's plan of salvation was fulfilled. His passion on the cross has officially made Jesus the bridge between us and God the Father. **We can reach God because of the sacrifice of Christ.** The cross becomes the official stepping stone for us to reach God. He is near you and has loved you with an everlasting love (Jeremiah 31:3). Sin has lost its power to separate us from the Father. Joy is again possible but it takes our **yes** for all this to happen. Salvation is indeed a free gift for us that comes with a great cost – the life of Jesus. It is entirely up to us if we want to accept this gift. How does this amazing gift of salvation affect our lives? Do we allow God to change us through Jesus Christ? Do we allow ourselves to be loved unconditionally?

Let's take a moment to be honest with ourselves. Which of the following is easier: writing ten good things about ourselves or writing ten things we do not like about ourselves? More often than not it is easier to recognise the things we do not like about ourselves. Like what I have shared earlier, I had tonnes of things that I didn't like about myself. Some of my complaints would sound like this: other girls were more popular, the guy I like seemed to like other girls; there must be something wrong with me; my body does not have the best shape; I was too fat in all the wrong areas of my body; my best friend gets more likes on Facebook; I hate my straight hair; I wished that my face is flawless; why can't I have her skin? These few were among the many things I complained daily about myself. I was so busy looking at my flaws that I could not see my worth. It was not possible for me to allow myself to be loved.

That was how I lived my life; with constant comparison and dissatisfaction. I am privileged that Christ found me and led me to find myself. As I mentioned earlier, falling in love with **Love** lead me to fall in love with myself. Only when I decided to make Jesus my only Lord and Saviour did I start to allow Him to love me unconditionally. Giving my life to Christ led me to an important question I asked myself: **Who am I?** This is the fundamental question that I encourage you to ask yourself. The outcome of our lives is centred upon our identity. People who are secure about themselves tend to be happier and more contented. As you seek to know more about yourself, the other very important question you need to ask is: **who are you, God?**

In our quest to find out about who we are, it is important

to have knowledge of God. The only way to God the Father is through Jesus, His Son. It means knowing Jesus. Invite Him into your heart and make Him your only Lord and Saviour. Jesus is the One who will tell you of your real worth. He is the Way, the Truth and the Life. He is the Good Shepherd that came to give you life, life to the fullest (John 10:10). He will give you a new perspective in life. Your circumstances may not change but your response would change to a more life giving one. Only when you build your identity on God's terms, we build our house upon the rock. Whatever the weather may be; you know that you stand on firm ground. You would be courageous to face any adversity that comes your way.

My experience in this has been one that is both fulfilling and humbling. Being a very capable person, I was put in a situation where all my talents and capabilities were not appreciated. If my identity had been built upon the works I do, I would have crumbled for a long time. Even though at that time I felt really useless, God showed me who I really was. My identity as the Beloved Daughter of God has helped me to see that God has the final say in who I am. It does not matter how the world around may label me, what matters most to me is what the Father says about me. I would like to invite you to examine who do you base your identity upon. Who has the final say about you?

A Masterpiece

So what does God really say about you? Here I would

encourage you to allow God to speak to you. Knowing in your heart that you have a Good Creator who loves you, what do you think He would say to you?

Here are some of the truths that God wants you to know:

1.   **You** are His Beloved Child (1 John 3:1)
2.   **You** are Precious, Honoured and Loved (Isaiah 43:4)
3.   **You** are the Delight of the Father (Zephaniah 3:17)
4.   **You** are dignified in His sight (Luke 15:22)
5.   **You** are chosen (John 15:16)
6.   He has a great plan for **you** (Jeremiah 29:11)
7.   He had **you** in mind before the foundation of the world (Ephesians 1:4)

These are just a few truths about you and you can find more in the Bible. It may take some time for these truths to become flesh in our life. However, it is very possible to live a happy and fulfilled Christian life. Some practical things that can help us to have our identity deeply rooted are as follows;

1. **Invest in yourself** with investment that will last for a lifetime.

• Attend youth camps or seminars that will help you in getting yourself rooted in your identity in Christ.

• Get yourself a mentor/spiritual director/spiritual accompanier/coach. A person whom you can be open with and someone you can trust. This person will support you in your journey of faith and will act

as a mirror for you. Having someone who would listen to you will help you to see things in different light

2. **Set daily appointments with Jesus** and have a good time chatting with Him. He loves hearing from you and He is ever ready to speak to you. Dedicating time for prayer makes a huge difference in our lives. **Be up for a surprisingly wonderful day when you decide to make time for prayer**. Prayer brings you closer to God and provides you with the grace to face the day.

3. Besides spending time with Jesus, **spend time knowing Him through the Scriptures** (check out Chapter 8). The Bible is the best resource you will ever have. Make it a point to invite the Holy Spirit every time you begin your Bible reading. It is after all God's Word speaking to ordinary folks and as we know, the BIBLE simple means: Basic Instructions Before Leaving Earth.

4. **Receive the Sacraments** as often as you can. The Body and Blood of Christ are the source and summit of our lives (check out Chapter 7). Receiving Communion often will strengthen us and the grace that comes with it is just simply awesome. Another Sacrament that helps our journey of faith would be the Sacrament of Reconciliation. It is a very beautiful Sacrament that heals us every time we receive it. Think about the time you went for a sincere confession, how do you feel after that? I believe it felt great and those great confession experiences were also indicators of the healing in your life that

is taking place. Know that it is God who administers the Sacraments through the hands of His priest. The master behind it all is God.

5. **Share your gifts**. It is through sharing that we receive much. If you are a painter, do something that glorifies God through your painting. If you sing well, sing to God. If you dance well, dance for Him. If you cook well, cook for Him. Keep sharing yourself and keep being a witness of Christ through your gifts.

When Jesus walked on the face of the earth, He was also on a journey of discovery. This is how He can relate fully to us. Can you imagine Jesus stating His destiny was to suffer, die on the cross and then rise from the dead on the third day when He was 12 years old? I would imagine that it may have freaked Him out if He understood it fully. He only started mentioning His Passion on the cross after the Transfiguration. The Gospel has shown to us that Jesus was also on a journey on earth and it was a very exciting journey of discovery and living that discovery. So dear friends, I would like to encourage you to take one thing at a time. At every juncture of self-discovery, thank and praise God for it. Whether this journey of life discovery is going to be an awesome one or otherwise, it is completely up to you. I pray that you will enjoy your adventure of embracing your original design – the Masterpiece you are. Who you are matters to God and it definitely matters to the world. May Jesus be with you and bless you in your adventure!

CHAPTER 11: HEARTS ABLAZE – SAINTHOOD
Luke Dowle

Luke has been a Liverpool supporter since he was five and this has him taught about patience and perseverance since their last league title was when he was two. He has been involved in youth missionary work with the ICPE mission teams in Germany, the USA and Malta.

Called to be Saints Together

What do you want to be when you are older? What people do you look up to? Who are your heroes? I'm sure we all have opinions on each of these questions and I'm sure they will vary a lot. However, how many of us when asked this question reply that we want to be a Saint? Probably not that many! We think this is just for the few people who are holy enough such as monks, nuns, priests, martyrs or even the Pope. It doesn't seem to be as exciting as being a professional sports player, a firefighter, a singer, a doctor, an astronaut or whatever we might be aspiring to be as an adult.

When I was younger I firstly wanted to be a footballer and to play for the England National team. This eventually changed to tennis and this took up most of my free time as a teenager. I then had to make the decision to go to university and my dream job changed again and again. But the one constant factor I have always had in my life is going to Church which evolved into a personal relationship with Christ when I was about seventeen.

When Pope Benedict XVI came to the UK for a Papal visit in 2010 I tried to go to as much of the visit as I possibly could. I had no idea how big the reception would be for him and I was blown away with the support he received. I had never been this close to a Pope and I could see him visibly touching many people.

The defining moment of the visit for me was the service held in Hyde Park in London where the youth were in the area closest to the Pope at the front. Having come from a small countryside parish with only a handful of youth it was incredible to see thousands of other young people who all shared the same faith. Towards the end of the service, the Pope led almost half an hour of adoration and the entire crowd of about one hundred thousand people went virtually silent for this whole period. It made me realise I was part of a much bigger Church than I had ever been aware of before.

Pope Benedict made a lot of time for the young people who he met outside of Westminster Cathedral and also gave a speech directed just to us. The words of the Pope struck me as he was inviting us all to be Saints. Yes, all of us! Reaching out to the youth the Pope said:

"I hope that among those of you listening to me today there are some of the future Saints of the twenty-first century. What God wants most of all for each one of you is that you should become holy.

He loves you much more than you could
ever begin to imagine, and He wants the
very best for you. And by far the best
thing for you is to grow in holiness.
Perhaps some of you have never thought
about this before. Perhaps some of you
think being a Saint is not for you. When I
invite you to become Saints, I am asking
you not to be content with second best. I
am asking you not to pursue one limited
goal and ignore all the others.

Having money makes it possible to be
generous and to do good in the world, but
on its own, it is not enough to make us
happy. Being highly skilled in some activity
or profession is good, but it will not satisfy
us unless we aim for something greater
still. It might make us famous, but it will
not make us happy.

Happiness is something we all want, but
one of the great tragedies in this world is
that so many people never find it, because
they look for it in the wrong places. The
key to it is very simple – true happiness is
to be found in God. We need to have the
courage to place our deepest hopes in God
alone, not in money, in a career, in worldly
success, or in our relationships with
others, but in God.

Only He can satisfy the deepest needs of
our hearts. You begin to feel compassion

for people in difficulties and you are eager
to do something to help them. You want
to come to the aid of the poor and the
hungry, you want to comfort the
sorrowful, you want to be kind and
generous. And once these things begin to
matter to you, you are well on the way to
becoming saints."

It is easy to not always put our deepest hopes in God, but Pope Benedict says that 'true happiness is to be found in God.' I don't know about you but this is something I really want! Jesus said that He "came that they may have life, and have it abundantly" (John 10:10). **Christianity is not a hindrance to our lives but will lead us to find fulfilment in it through Jesus.** This isn't just for a select few, we are **all** being called.

Set Apart

In fact, we are told that as Christians, "he who called you is holy, be holy yourselves in all your conduct" (1 Peter 1:15). Since all of us are called to be holy, then we are **all** part of the 'Communion of Saints' which we hear about every time we go to Church. The YouCat (146) says this is comprised of:

"...all men who have placed their
hope in Christ and belong to Him through
Baptism, whether they have already died or

> are still alive. Because in Christ we are one
> Body; we live in a communion that
> encompasses heaven and earth."

This means that to qualify for being a Saint all we need is to be baptised. And not only that we are called to be Saints whilst we are still alive on earth!

Therefore we are part of the Communion of Saints which include some of the Church's greatest ones such as St Peter, St Paul, St Francis of Assisi, St Catherine of Siena, St Padre Pio, St Thérèse of Lisieux and then at the end we can add our own name.

I was blessed to be able to go to World Youth Day Madrid in 2011. This is a global gathering of young Catholics with the Pope for a celebration of the amazing faith we share. After experiencing the Papal Visit in London I thought I had some idea of what it might be like. Yet again God surprised me! For those who have been to a World Youth Day you will know what I am talking about, but for those who haven't, you really need to try to go to one as you never know quite what it is like until you experience it.

The first thing I noticed was that there were a lot of young people in Madrid to see the Pope, and I mean a lot! When we went to the opening Mass, we were over two streets away from where the Pope was but it didn't matter as there were big screens everywhere and everyone was joyful. Later in the evening we found out that over two million people had gone to that Mass! I carried a British flag around with our group as there were people from nearly every country in the world there and the amount of people who wanted photos with us was amazing. Sadly selfie-sticks weren't yet a thing! Often we couldn't even communicate in the same language but that seemed to matter less and less as it was our faith that united us. We are **all** "**called to be saints,** together with **all** those who in **every place** call on the name of our Lord Jesus Christ" (1 Corinthians 1:2, emphasis added).

Attraction of the Saints

As my faith journey continues I have become more interested in the lives of the Saints canonised by the Church who are recognised as people who lived extraordinary lives for Christ and are in heaven interceding to God on our behalf in a powerful way. They are also our brothers and sisters in Christ and are part of the same 'Communion of Saints' as we are. In the letter to the Hebrews (12:1, emphasis added) it says:

"Therefore, since we are surrounded by
so great a **cloud of witnesses**,
let us also lay aside every weight and the
sin that clings so closely,
and let us run with perseverance the race
that is set before us".

This refers to us being surrounded by the Saints who have gone before us and they are there to cheer us on to the victory of heaven and eternal life with God. **They are an**

inspiration and through their examples of faith they encourage us to persevere in our own race. Since God has created each of us uniquely, all of our races will differ but we all have the same finish line in sight.

Hebrews 12:1 sets us the challenge to 'lay aside every weight and the sin that clings so closely'. **God wants us to be set apart and holy.** 2 Timothy 2:21 says:

> "All those who cleanse themselves
> of the things I have mentioned
> will become special utensils,
> dedicated and useful to the owner of the
> house, ready for every good work."

This isn't something that happens overnight and is something we need to constantly work on. It is only through the grace of God, a personal relationship with Jesus and the continual presence and guidance of the Holy Spirit that we can become holy. We can't do it in our own strength. Each day we need to ask the Holy Spirit to help us.

However, we are not alone if we struggle. Through the lives of the Saints it is clear that they also struggled just like us! Peter who was chosen to lead the early Church (Matthew 16:18) denied Jesus three times despite saying, "Even though I must die with you, I will not deny you" (Matthew 26:35). Paul before his conversion on the road to Emmaus "was ravaging the church by entering house after house; dragging off both men and women, he committed them to prison" (Acts 8:3). He was persecuting Christians yet became one of the Church's greatest ever Saints. The list could go on, but I have found that different Saints seem to find us when we need particular guidance or help in our journeys of faith.

Saint Padre Pio of Pietrelcina (1887-1968)

The Litany of the Saints prayed at the Easter vigil is an incredible list of Holy men, women and Angels in the Church. Saints have come through all periods of history and through different situations which helps to make them all unique. Despite knowing the names of many Saints I had never taken a lot of time to learn more about them, so although this part of the Easter Vigil was always interesting, I didn't know much more about the names I was reciting.

Whilst at University my fascination with the Saints started to grow and my brother spoke about one in particular called Padre Pio who I hadn't heard about before. He told me that this Saint had the stigmata (which are the five wounds of Christ: the feet, the hands and His side), could bilocate (being in two physical places at the same time) and God used him to bring many miracles[3]! I was so intrigued, that as soon as I got home to my laptop I had to learn more about Padre Pio.

The first thing I gathered was that there was a huge

[3] I recognise that the Catholic Church has not definitively accepted the physical Bilocation of the Saints, and some Catholic philosophers and theologians have argued against it in the Church's history. Nevertheless, these dramatic and inspiring stories point us, at least, to the Spiritual closeness that the Saints and Holy People have to us, and what a great comfort it is for us to believe in the Communion of the Saints.

amount written about the stigmata and the gift of bilocation: it really was true. The amazing thing I found with Padre Pio was that he only died in 1968, with many people alive today having met him before he died! I was so excited about Padre Pio that I had to buy a book on his life straight away and couldn't stop telling my friends and family about him. I really felt Padre Pio had found me at this point of my life.

The story about his stigmata is worth discovering in full, but it ultimately came from his life of prayer when he desired to identify with the crucified Christ and to offer himself to God for the salvation of mankind. Padre Pio never wanted the visible wounds and even asked his priest Fr Pannullo to 'ask Jesus to take them away'.

Very few Saints in history have had the stigmata and not one as well documented as Padre Pio. Others who are known to have had them are St Francis of Assisi and St Catherine of Siena. Padre Pio used to hide the stigmata as much as he could. He would always wear gloves to try and disguise them but this was hard as they would bleed so much. The stigmata was constant throughout Padre Pio's life until he died and they vanished. Every Easter during Holy Week the stigmata would hurt more than normal to coincide with the Passion of Christ and there are many witnesses of this.

Another aspect of Padre Pio's life was the special gift of bilocation where a person can be in two places at once. It is a mysterious gift that cannot be fully explained and seems to be way beyond human understanding, but we must remember nothing is impossible for God (Matthew 19:26). Bilocation has been given to a few Saints but Padre Pio's accounts of it occurring are the most documented. Often this gift is given by God for when it is physically impossible for a Saint to be present somewhere under normal circumstances. It was known for Padre Pio to be praying in the Monastery at San Giovanni Rotondo in Italy and not be aware of the people around him as he was in another place at the same time. It was well known that Padre Pio didn't travel much, especially when he was in San Giovanni Rotondo, yet there are accounts of people being with him from all over the world including in the USA, South America, and the UK: all places he had never visited.

The most documented case occurred during World War II when Padre Pio appeared in the air in front of American bomber planes who were going to attack the city of San Giovanni Rotondo. The pilots later remarked that they saw a brown robed friar with outstretched arms and no matter how hard they tried to release the weapons, the bombs failed to drop. Padre Pio had promised the citizens of the town before this that they would be spared and he kept the promise! The American pilots later came back to the town when an allied airbase was set up at Foggia just a few miles away. They immediately went to the monastery to see if a monk was there who looked like the one who appeared to the air. To their immense surprise they recognised Padre Pio and it wasn't part of their imagination!

In fact, Padre Pio just replied to the Commanding General Nathan Twining 'so you are the one that wanted to destroy everything!' Understandingly, the General had a massive conversion experience becoming close friends with the friar and I am sure many of the other pilots who saw Padre Pio did too.

Remarkably, this is only one story of the many miracles occurring with Padre Pio bilocating and if it has excited you as much as it did me about the power of God then I would definitely read more about this incredible Saint as there are many other miracles attributed to him during his life and after he died.

Remember Padre Pio is part of the same 'Communion of Saints' that we are and he is cheering us on in our race too. We can ask him to pray for us as just as we can ask any of our friends or family around us. Below is a prayer that many people use when asking Padre Pio for his intercession, maybe before praying it, you could think of something on your heart that you would like St Padre Pio's prayers for:

Dear God, You generously blessed Your servant,
St. Pio of Pietrelcina,
with the gifts of the Spirit.
You marked his body with the five wounds
of Christ Crucified, as a powerful witness
to the saving Passion and Death of Your Son.
Endowed with the gift of discernment,
St. Pio laboured endlessly in the confessional
for the salvation of souls.
With reverence and intense devotion
in the celebration of Mass,
he invited countless men and women
to a greater union with Jesus Christ
in the Sacrament of the Holy Eucharist.

Through the intercession of St. Pio of
Pietrelcina,
I confidently beseech You to grant me
the grace of (here state your petition).

Glory be to the Father... (three times).
Amen.

Steps to Sainthood

Hopefully you have become inspired by the example of
Saint Padre Pio and want to tell others about how God used
him! Other Saints lived equally incredible lives. Saints that have
inspired me include Saint Catherine of Siena and Saint Teresa
of Ávila. Both of them are greatly loved Saints in the Church
and amazing examples to us today even though they lived
hundreds of years ago.

Saint Catherine was born into a large family in the 14th
century and being a woman was not expected to have a
massive impact in a male dominated society. Like Padre Pio
she was known to have the stigmata and an important scene in
her life was the mystical marriage to Christ which is depicted in
many paintings particularly during the Renaissance. One of the
most remarkable achievements of Saint Catherine was
convincing Pope Gregory XI to return the papacy from
Avignon (in France) to Rome after an exile of the papacy of
almost 70 years. She believed that it was only right for the
Pope to be in Rome, and the fact that Pope Gregory took her

seriously as a woman in this period shows the influence Catherine had. It helps us to realise that God can use each one of us to fulfill His purpose if we allow Him to use us.

Saint Teresa of Ávila is also a great example to us today. She helped to reform the Carmelite Order and is famous for her writings such as the book 'Interior Castle'. She famously struggled with prayer which wasn't a massive part of her life until she was 41 years old. Yet she is now one of the most famous Saints who wrote about prayer! She spoke about perseverance, as through this God will give us blessings beyond our expectations.

Prayer can be something that we all struggle with at some point and it is encouraging that a Saint like Teresa did also! It shows us that the Saints really were normal people like us today. In fact Teresa wasn't meant to communicate with many people when she was part of the Carmelites but she just had to write to and hear from her friends. One of her friends who she kept in contact a lot with was Saint John of the Cross! Teresa is a very relatable character with a real heart for God and someone who wants to encourage us in our journey with Christ. One of her most famous prayers is the following and is worth remembering:

Let nothing trouble you,

Let nothing make you afraid.

All things pass away.

God never changes.

Patience obtains everything.

God alone is enough.

Once we realise that we are part of the same 'Communion of Saints' as people like Padre Pio, Catherine of Siena and Teresa of Ávila, it should really excite us! By being baptised Christians we have a massive family, and a family that increases every day. The great thing about being part of a family is that there are always members there to pick us up when we fall or when we are feeling down. Likewise we can help others when they need our help.

Pope Benedict XVI realises that Sainthood needs to become the norm in our society and something every young person strives for. We can start by recognising those who have gone before us in faith and learn more about their lives and how they can help us today to grow closer to God as after all they are part of the 'cloud of witnesses' cheering us on towards the finish line (Hebrews 12:1).

There are many ways that we can grow in our journeys towards Sainthood. However we are all unique and each of us has a different journey. The following are examples that we can all use in our journey that I have found useful:

- **Scripture** - immersing ourselves in the living and active Word of God.

- **Perseverance -** just like Saint Teresa we need to persevere even if we feel far away from God as He is still there.

- **Patience** - learning that everything is in God's timing and not ours.

- **Prayer** - the key to any relationship with God.

- **Intercession** - like asking friends and family to pray for us, we can also turn to the Saints of the Church such as Mother Mary, Padre Pio, Catherine of Siena and Teresa of Ávila.

- **Sacraments** - a constant use of the Sacraments will help us to grow, this includes the Eucharist and the Sacrament of Reconciliation.

- **Holy Spirit** - we can always turn to the Holy Spirit to guide us as this is a gift Jesus gave to us to help us to grow closer to Him.

- **Friends** - make sure we have people around us who will help us in our journey to Sainthood. If there are negative people around us or those who are hindering us, then we need to think about whether they are good friends for us in our journey. On the other hand, if someone is full of joy and the gifts of the Spirit (Galatians 5:22-23) then we should want to spend more time with them!

- **Spiritual director** - having someone who we can speak to and ask advice from. This can be a priest, a nun or someone we look up to on our spiritual journey.

Lastly, we need to realise that we will make mistakes and we will fall short, but it is how we respond that will ultimately shape our journey of faith.

"The steadfast love of the LORD never ceases, his mercies never come to an end; they are **new every morning**" (Lamentations 3:22-23, emphasis added).

Sainthood isn't just any journey, it is a journey drawing us to our Heavenly Father who created us, the God who loves us unconditionally and gave His Son to die for us so that might live (John 3:16). Jesus wants us to have life, and "have it abundantly" (John 10:10).

Sainthood is something to get excited about! We are all called to it no matter where we are from or what has happened in our lives to far. Saint Catherine of Siena famously said, 'Be who God meant you to be and you will set the world on fire' and this is the impact that we as Saints will have on the world and those around us. Let's set our aims high with our eyes fixed on Jesus, and together as the 'Communion of Saints' we will set the world on fire.

Want to know more?

- Padre Pio Man of Hope - Renzo Allegri
- Teresa of Ávila An Extraordinary Life - Shirley du Boulay
- Catherine of Siena - Sigrid Undset
- Interior Castle - Teresa of Ávila
- Angels and Saints: A Biblical Guide to Friendship with God's Holy Ones - Scott Hahn

CHAPTER 12: CONSTRUCTION SITE – ENCOURAGEMENT
Lewis Dowle

God has a handmade, irreplaceable, one-of-a-kind blueprint of our lives. A masterpiece which He has hand-built, brick by brick with Christ as our Cornerstone (1 Peter 2:7). Any of us who have played with LEGO or sandcastles know that buildings aren't always stable. Things can come up as opposition to them. It could be our little sister pretending to be Godzilla (again), or our neighbour's dog destroying a sandcastle. Not every building that *we* make is strong enough to withstand Baby Godzilla or Destructo the Dog. But every building that Christ makes *is* strong enough because He is the foundation.

Our words can help play a big role in the life of the buildings of others. Think of it like Jenga. When we speak to others, we have the choice to either build them up or, like Jenga, take a piece from them to make their building less stable.

The Bible talks about our lives as buildings, namely a house and a temple. In 1 Corinthians 6:19-20, St Paul talks about our body being the 'temple of the Holy Spirit'. Jesus talks about our lives as a house:

"Everyone then who hears these words of mine and acts on them will be **like a wise**

man who built his house on rock. The
rain fell, the floods came, and the winds
blew and beat on that house, **but it did
not fall, because it had been founded
on rock**. And everyone who hears these
words of mine and does not act on them
will be like a foolish man who built his
house on sand. The rain fell, and the
floods came, and the winds blew and beat
against that house, and it fell—
and great was its fall!"
(Matthew 7:24-27, emphasis added)

We as Christians have Christ as our Foundation. He is the 'Rock' on which we are called to build our lives. The rain, flood and wind hit both houses in Jesus' parable, both the Christians and the non-Christians. But what happened? Those who built their life on Jesus were strong and standing after the storm, and the others were in a very tricky situation!

Storms are going to come against us. They are like wrecking-balls on a destruction site. They can come swinging in and destroy their prey. Wrecking-balls can trash buildings, cars and towers. To us they can be negative words spoken by teachers, difficult family situations, or people trying to push themselves over us. Nothing can stop the wrecking-ball. Well, that isn't quite true actually.

You see, with Christ as our Cornerstone, our Foundation, the One on whom we build our lives, sure the wrecking-ball is going to come, it is likely to hit us even more as Christians. But here's the cool thing. **We are built on Rock.** When we are rooted in Christ, though things hit us, they don't need to tear us down. If someone comes with a wrecking-ball, we don't need to allow it to affect us. Jesus is our Protector and that means He is, well...our Protector!

> "You who live in shelter of the Most High,
> who abide in the shadow of the Almighty,
> will say to the LORD,
> **'My refuge and my fortress**;
> my God, in whom I trust'"
> (Psalm 90:1-2 [91:1-2], emphasis added).

We do not need to allow the wrecking-ball to tear us down every time it swings at us. We can build our lives on Christ.

In the same way others can speak over our lives and choose to either help the building grow higher or use a wrecking-ball to tear it down, so too do we have that power. God says how He sets before us a choice of life or death (Deuteronomy 30:15), so choose life! We choose life every time we encourage someone, every time we congratulate the team who beat us, every time we choose to look at someone's strengths rather than their weaknesses. We should aim to encourage others, Christians and non-Christians alike. Not only do our kind words make life more enjoyable for all, they can even be used to lead people to Jesus. But we will come back to this later in the chapter.

We first need to think about how we can build our lives on the Rock. It is easy for us to say, how can I encourage someone when I feel so discouraged myself? Well I think it is time you get yourself a hot drink, a nice chair and an open heart, because this section is all about that.

Dream Big

God want us to be encouraged. When people encourage us, we feel electric, we feel a buzz.

"I want their hearts to be encouraged and united in love" (Colossians 2:2).

When God made you, He didn't create you to be 'average'. He created you to excel, to live life to the full (John 10:10). He created you to be a Saint. He made you perfectly: you're a living masterpiece!

Artwork can sell for millions of pounds. It's not what the painting is of necessarily, **it is who the artist is.** We are invaluable because our Artist is God! I heard a story about Lecrae (a Christian rapper) who went shopping in Beverly Hills. He wanted to pick up a t-shirt whilst he was there, so decided to visit a shop. After looking through some tops, he found one he quite liked. He looked at the price and, a little taken aback, noticed a label of hundreds of dollars! He then discovered it was on the sales rack! Perplexed he spoke to the shopping assistant asking what material it was made of. Plainly the man replied cotton. The guy couldn't believe how just a plain cotton shirt was so expensive! The shop assistant said, "You see, it's not what the material is made of. It is that price because of the designer. It is because of who's name is on it." It is the same with you and I. We are precious, we are invaluable because our Designer is our Heavenly Father!

> "Be who God meant you to be and you
> will set the world on fire"
> (St Catherine of Sienna).

However, so often people speak down to us, especially to us as young people. Don't ever accept words spoken negatively against you. Here we can learn from the profound words of Taylor Swift: **Shake it off!** When people criticise your hair, tell you that you're not smart enough or that you're too young, just shake it off!

> "If anyone will not welcome you or listen
> to your words, **shake off the dust** from
> your feet as you leave that house or town"
> (Matthew 10:14, emphasis added).

So many people try and place baggage on us, they leave us with dust on our feet. But Jesus says to us just as He said to the disciples: **Shake off the dust**. As God calls us to different things, we can't bring with us the dust (e.g. the negative words someone spoke to us) of the last place to the new things He is calling us to. **We need to start fresh**. God is making all things new, so anything not from Him we need to shake off and then press on (Revelations 21:5)! Words can bring a lot of good, but they can also prevent us from what God is calling us to do in life. Just as we sort the post in the morning as to what we should keep or throw out, so too we must be careful which words we welcome or not.

There were once two authors. One of them had been working on a book series and decided to show it to his friend. His friend wasn't convinced. So much so, the author decided to leave the book on the bookshelf for years. Do you know what the book series was? It was The Chronicles of Narnia and the friend was J.R.R. Tolkien, the author of The Lord of the Rings. Tolkien and C.S. Lewis were close friends, however because of Tolkien's words, Narnia almost never left the wardrobe.

Sometimes, with good intentions people say things to us, they try to quell our dreams. It is important for us to listen to those want the best for us, but some people don't want to see our dreams come to pass. They see us as balloons which they keep trying to prevent from flying away, they see in us the potential to take to the skies.

> "God would not have put a dream in your heart if He hadn't already given you everything you need to fulfill it"
> (Joel Osteen).

What ultimately matters is what God says about you, and what plans He has for your life. One of my favourite Bible verses is from Jeremiah:

> "For surely I know the plans I have for
> you, says the LORD, plans for your
> welfare and not for harm, to give you a
> future with a hope"
> (Jeremiah 29:11).

God has placed dreams in our heart. These dreams are like a campfire. To build a fire, we first need some dry wood, but we also need a **spark.** Something to set the fire ablaze. Our words, actions and responses are that spark. They can also be rain however. But here's the point: the wood is already there. Everything is set up for an incredible bonfire to roast your marshmallows. **But we need the spark.** God has set up the wood for the fire, but sometimes ourselves or others dampen the wood and rain off the party.

It's time to get your viva back. Dream big. God wouldn't put a dream in your heart unless he had a purpose for it. Dream to be the world's best footballer, a composer, a doctor, the President, a priest, an astronaut, a mother, a pilot. The very fact that you are breathing is a sign that God loves you and that He has a plan for your life! You can do it. You can do all things through Christ who gives you strength (Philippians 4:13). The trick is this, to not only dream at night, but also in the day.

Dream Together

Who we spend time with is also vital. It is very easy to feel discouraged if we spend our whole time with Upset Olli and Sad Sally! We can't always control the words spoken to us, but we can choose our friends.

"Iron sharpens iron, and one person
sharpens the wits of another"
(Proverbs 27:17).

We are each created to be a Saint, but this often doesn't happen alone. There is strength in numbers! Lots of saints came in pairs or groups, they encouraged each other, they challenged each other and they prayed for each other. For example St Francis and St Claire; St Peter and St Paul; St John Bosco and St Dominic Savio; St Teresa of Ávila and St John of the Cross, and Blessed Mother Teresa and St John Paul II. Just as a fish can only grow up to the limiting size of the pond, to too can we set limits on ourselves by the friends we spend time with.

A change in friendship groups is never instant or easy, but it is often better to have a few close friends who encourage us, than lots of people who perhaps aren't genuine or have our best interests at heart. Without realising it, we can be led down paths we don't want to take. If we don't have Christians around us, we can pray. We can ask Jesus to bring the right friends into our lives.

An Instruction Manual Please!

There is huge power in encouragement, it is a vessel which God uses to pour His grace into our lives. Just one smile or one sentence can completely change someone's day of rain into the finest summer's afternoon! Have you ever noticed that when you walk into a room smiling, the atmosphere changes. It brings fun, life and God's love into the room.

> "Let no one ever come to you without leaving better and happier. Be the living expression of God's kindness: kindness in your face, kindness in your eyes, kindness in your smile"
> (Saint Mother Teresa).

Mother T's words are powerful. "Let **no one**" come away not feeling better off and happier after spending time with us. What if we as Christians put this into practice! The power would shake the very foundation of the world. Imagine if every Christian in the world lived like this. If each of us used words to encourage others and to smile at the people around us?

> "Joy, which is like the sign of a Christian. A Christian without joy is either not a Christian or he is sick. There's no other type!" (Pope Francis)

Many times we will be at Mass and joyful may not be the words we use to describe our parishes! But it is what we are called to. **Be the spark.** By God's grace we can be the light to change that. As young people, we have a great privilege on many levels, and one of them is the ability to draw comments from older people! Let's live our lives like St Timothy in the New Testament, where we as young people set the example:

"Let no one despise your youth, but **set the believers an example** in speech and conduct, in love, in faith, in purity" (1 Timothy 4:12, emphasis added).

Let's lead lives which are contagious: **joy is contagious**. Have you ever spent time with someone who makes you smile even before they have said anything? It draws you to that person.

When leading our friends to know God and His love for each of us, sometimes to draw them in isn't easy. Some teens have misconceptions about God which they've heard from either the TV or their family. But being a positive person, someone who smiles and encourages other people, will draw them to the very source of all these good things: the Holy Spirit inside us. There is no joy apart from God.

By our words and smiles, we become living magnets. Are we repelling the world or are our those around us drawn to God's Holy Spirit alive in us? Christianity is not boring. Just look at Pope Francis if anyone ever tells you that! Pope Francis has caused a media storm, everyone is fascinated by him.

Father Stan Fortuna (CFR) talks about Fascination and Attraction. How our lives as Christians are meant to fascinate others, to attract others. If someone looks at a Christian and they don't seem full of joy, they are unlikely to want to find out more about God. Our non-Christian brothers and sisters want what Christians have. Namely Jesus! Jesus is love, Jesus is joy, Jesus is peace, Jesus is kindness, Jesus is goodness (Galatians 5:22-23).

Being British, of course I love Her Majesty the Queen. Queen Elizabeth II has been our monarch for decades and decades. Despite being in her late 80s, she has this amazing habit, and it's the same as what Mother T said: not leaving people without encouraging them or offering a kind word. How do we as young people grow in this amazing gift? Some of us may find it easier than others, but remember, joy is contagious! Have you ever been with someone who is absolutely passionate at something which is really quite unusual?

I have a friend who is crazy about butterflies and moths. He absolutely loves them. He tells everyone how good looking they are. He knows everything about them. He goes to special conventions. He sets up humane traps to record them. He is (this is a real word) a lepidopterist! Before meeting him I never really gave butterflies or moths much attention, **but passion is contagious**. I found myself getting excited when I saw a butterfly on a walk, always associating them with my friend. I've even been known to photograph them on my phone!

Another time I found myself with two seaweed specialists (it's a long story!). Having never thought about the seaweed world in great detail before, I watched these two people with a passion for seaweed find an incredible diversity of seaweed. Over forty species found in a two-hour scout! Again, it makes you look at something differently when you spend time with someone who is passionate about it. I now associate sea-weeds with that day!

Imagine someone saying that about us as the Church! Imagine that when people see a Catholic young person, they instantly associate joy, love, smiles and hope with us! That's quite an awesome picture. A great way to achieve this challenge is through encouragement. To encourage is a verb. A word with action. It is dynamic and essential to the Christian life. Here are four ways we can make it a part of our everyday life.

1. **As with every good gift, it comes from God.** We can do no good deed without the grace of God. God loves us and His children so much that when we come to Him, He pours countless gifts and blessings into our lives. God is the source of our encouragement. We can't give what we don't have. If you're looking for things to be thankful for, check out Chapter 3! When we spend time thanking God for all His countless blessings, we can't help but smile and encourage those around us!

2. **Spend time with upbeat people.** Proverbs 27:17 talks about iron sharpening iron and how our friends work in the same way. We need to be surrounded by people who encourage us, people who challenge us to

rise higher, to help us aspire to be the Saints God is calling us to become.

From here we can go out into the world to bring God's love and His kindness to all His children. But first we need the strength of close friends to support us. Bear Grylls (a fantastic Christian role-model) was part of Britain's secret forces, the elite of the elite, the S.A.S. In the S.A.S. they often operate in fours. Enough people to be close to, but not too many to make the mission difficult to operate. If you were asked to pick an elite team of your closest friends, who would they be? As we dream big, we need people who will dream with us.

To encourage people, we also need to be encouraged ourselves. Upbeat friends can give us a strength to share God's message of love with others. Spending time with people who aren't excited about life can be tiring, but those who have a passion for life fill us with a buzz, especially time with God Himself.

3. **Keeping an eye on our tongues.** Not physically. That would be weird. Our words are crucial to living the Christian life. We wouldn't be great witnesses to Christ if we go around complaining the whole time or bringing negativity into our conversation. The words we speak are powerful. If we spend our whole time telling ourselves "I'll never be good at Maths" or "Coach says I'll never be good enough to play for the team", chances are if we don't change our words we

won't be! The evangelist Joyce Meyer says how 'Where the mouth goes, the man follows'. Think of our words as laying tracks for a train. When we speak, we lay the down the track in front of us and our lives are the trains. But which direction the train goes depends on the tracks we place.

4. **Smile, smile and then smile some more!** This is probably the easiest but one of the most powerful forms of encouragement. St Thérèse of Lisieux, a Doctor of the Church said:

"A word or a smile is often enough to put fresh life in a despondent soul."

When we're ordering at Starbucks, when we get our essay back, when someone lends us a pen, :D :D :D! **Smiles make people smile**. We don't always have to feel like smiling to share one with someone. Even if we've had a tough day, chances are there will be something we can smile about! Smiles also draw people to us. This is so important for evangelisation. Through our smiles we may be able to start a conversation which otherwise may not have happened. If people know we are a Christian and we spend all our time smiling, they are going to say to us, "When can I come to Church with you!" Our friends long for the happiness that Jesus gives to us.

"Dear young people, the **happiness** you are seeking, the **happiness** you have a right to enjoy has a name and a face: it is Jesus of Nazareth, hidden in the Eucharist" (Pope Bendict XVI).

Ready, Set, Go!

Let's set ourselves a challenge. Let's encourage someone today. Whether it is someone at school, or our younger sister who's struggling with her homework, or thanking the postman, or smiling at the shop assistant. Have you ever seen loads of dominos all stacked up next to each other, where if you just knock the first one over it knocks all the following ones down? The effort to tip the first domino is so small, yet it mounts up to the huge and exciting show of all the dominos falling. **Let's start the domino chain**.

Let's go and encourage our friends. Smile at our teachers. Find a Bible verse for our cousin. Facebook message our brothers to say we're proud of them. Tweet a positive message to the world.

"The future starts today, not tomorrow."
(St Pope John Paul II)

So what are we waiting for? Ready? Set? **"Go therefore and make disciples of all nations"** (Matthew 28:19, emphasis added)!

CHAPTER 13: LIVE THE CALL – BEYOND SURVIVAL
Derek Chong

Derek is a professional life coach, from Sabah, Malaysia. He serves people through one-on-one coaching, giving training and leading workshops on self-awareness, communication and leadership. He is also the author of the book "30 days to a Better Self Awareness".

God has incredible plans for all of us. The God that Jesus revealed to us is a God who goes beyond our perspective of what we consider to be great, fantastic, awesome or good. As it is written in the book of Isaiah 55:8-9:

> "For my thoughts are not your thoughts,
> nor are your ways my ways,
> says the LORD.
> For as the heavens are higher than the
> earth, so are my ways higher than your
> ways, my thoughts higher than your
> thoughts."

Whatever God does, it is greater than our wildest imagination of love, kindness, generosity, humility and power. If we believe in this God, who created us, we will also come to realise who we are, the created. God made us in His likeness. God is love. **When we love, we come alive**. God blesses. When we live as a blessing to others, we find joy and fulfilment. God is great and I believe that until we see ourselves as incredible people and live out that greatness in us, we will not find life. We will live a life of mediocrity with a deep dissatisfaction and emptiness. The good news is that this was never God's plan. He has always had greater things in store for us.

Do you believe that God has a great plan for your life? Many Catholics that I have met believe in a semi-good life and plan a manageable lifestyle when it comes to living a life with Jesus Christ. Very few of us actually think that it is great, and even fewer dare to live out that greatness. Life is good, don't get me wrong. However, when we settle for what we think is good and miss the great inheritance that is graciously given by God the Father, we will never know who God is, who we truly are and we will not be free or alive. God's design is that we flourish, expand and grow. Let us take a few moments to consider what is God's great plan and how we can commit to this journey of living a great life.

A Change of Mindset

Why is being just good not good enough for us? Because living 'just good' is not God's plan. When we do not live according to God's plan, we live in a lie. A lie does not bring us freedom, truth does! With freedom, we learn to choose wisely, with love - which is the absence of pressure, manipulation or fear. Most of the time, we settle for something because we think that it is as good as it gets. But we are not settled when we know that there is something better. If life can be better than how it is right now, why should we settle for anything less? When our hope is that of making it through to the next day in one piece, that we will not get too stressed out and end up in ruins, then, that is exactly what we will experience in life.

What if I were to tell you that you can live life loving it, ending up great, happy, fulfilled, growing to be a significant person who will contribute to society, bringing joy and meaning to others and sharing the Gospel effectively to people in the world? Would you settle for less? We see this natural response from toddlers. No toddler will settle for crawling because they know that they will one day walk and run. What has happened that so many of us are settling for less and abandoning the wonderful and great plans God has for us?

The Truths of God

The first thing we want to look at is our image of God. Is our God a wonderful God? Does He mean well for us? Are His plans and intensions the best for us? These have been the questions from the beginning of the human race. When Adam and Eve believed that God meant well for them, they lived in union with God and life was wonderful. When they doubted and thought that God was hiding something good from them, they took things into their own hands. Jesus, as the new Adam, revealed the greatness of God through His life and showed us that God has always had a great plan for us. He lived His life on earth in trust, love and service. We are called to trust Him completely because His goodness is ultimate. He has the best plan for our lives.

When we think of the true love of God, we naturally fall in love. How do you see God today? How does God desire to reveal Himself to you today?

Re-examine Who We Are

The second reality we want to take a look at is our identity. Who are you? When you give some answers to that question, how do you feel about those answers? Is there a deep conviction? When we come to know God, something that naturally follows is that we come to know our true self. When we see God rightly, we will hear Him rightly. Our God is a God of revelation. Throughout the centuries, He continues to make Himself known to us. God wants to be known, and calls us to love and serve Him.

As it is with God, when we are known for who we truly are, we are happy, we come alive and become more human. We were not created to be alone. People who prefer not to have close relationships with others can act this way sometimes as a result of being previously hurt. But when we dare to move beyond the pain and step into the light of being known again, life enters in. Being in the light is the better place to live. We want to be known.

I reckon that primarily, you are great, fantastic, awesome, incredible, fascinating, marvellous, brilliant, just to name a few. As we are created in the likeness of God, we reflect the truths of God. How do you see yourself today? When you ask God who you are in His eyes, what do you hear?

Connecting with our Call

When we know who we are in Christ, awesome thoughts and great dreams come to us. Often, they seem like crazy and extreme ideas. I believe that this is quite natural. **It mirrors who God is, in the sense that He is extreme while remaining true, great while remaining humble and out of this world while connected to us.** For many, the God of the Christians is so great and awesome that it seems absurd to them. They might be right to some extent, that there is actually nothing ordinary about God. He is extra-ordinary. So are His people. Our call is extra-ordinary. How will we know that these great dreams are from God and not just some crazy ideas?

1. **Do I love dearly?** Humans are made to respond to love. We want our response to God's great plans to

come out of the great love we have for Him. When we love God, we will also love His people. As Christians, we are called to respond out of love. Allow yourself to fall in love with God as you come to know Him more. Out of this great love for God, great dreams will be born.

2. **Is my dream connected to my passion?** Do I know what I am passionate about? It may be something I do, some people I love, or a particular topic that excites me. I would want my dream to be connected to this passion.

3. **Do I know my core values?** A part of self-discovery is that we connect to our values. We know what is important for us. When our conscience is clear, we filter all our plans through these values. We do not like to compromise them. When we do, it hurts us badly and sets us at war within ourselves. Whatever your dreams are, are they in line with your core set of values? If you find yourself justifying more than agreeing, you may want to double-check those dreams. Talk to someone to think it through.

4. **Does my dream serve people?** If God has made us to seek Him, know Him, love Him and serve Him, our dream will bear this significance. Everything we do is governed by these principles (of knowing, loving and serving). Wanting to be rich, to be the boss, or to have an easy life cannot be the ultimate reason for our dreams. We need to ask ourselves if what we do serves

God and His people. If it brings only temporary pleasure to ourselves while exploiting and hurting others, I assure you, no life or happiness can be found in such a dream. **We are designed to bring love, hope, joy and freedom through who we are and the way we live.** God will be glorified through the dreams that you have. Dreams such as these will bring us ultimate fulfillment.

5. **It is beyond us!** The plan of God is normally so great that when we imagine it, a part of us is filled with wonder and awe while another part of us is filled with fear. It is not the fear of being afraid but that of a deep knowing that we cannot do this on our own. Only with the grace of God, are we able to accomplish the dreams God has placed in our hearts. We feel honoured to be part of His awesome plan.

Live Your Call

The next logical step of having a great dream is to live it out. **Living out our dreams will reinforce your beliefs and faith in God.** It makes perfect sense that when we believe in a great God who has a great plan, living out that plan will result in ultimate goodness. It is unreasonable that we should know a great God and live a life that is miserable, unexciting or unfulfilled. So then, go ahead and start today. **Heaven starts on earth for those who believe in Christ because we live towards it.** Everything we do becomes a contribution towards building the dreams God has placed in our hearts. Living our lives apart from His plans tells us that we have some problems with the true image of God. Without the foundation, a wonderful fulfilled life cannot be built.

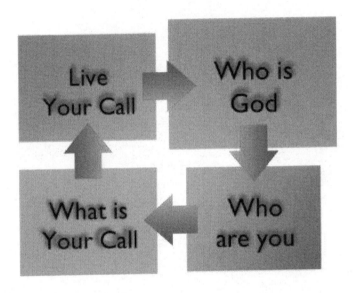

If I know the plan of God, what can I do today to contribute to that great plan? Every destination starts with the first step, then the next and so on until we get there. For some of us, it could be about learning through studying, training, rehearsing, reading or anything that helps us to improve and come closer to fulfill God's dreams in us. For others, it could be to simply start doing it, gaining experiences along the way. For example, if the dream is to preach, then start preaching. Be open for good feedback and learn from it. The more you do, the better you get. The more effective you are, the more people will benefit from your service.

Conclusion

Our lives were designed to be great. That greatness can start today. As Christians, the joy and fulfillment of the journey is part and parcel of the greatness of our destination. To live (at any age) is to grow in the knowledge of who God is, who you are, what your call is and live it out. If we desire to be alive, we must look beyond our survival plans and envisage the incredible plans of God. Since it is not God's plan that we simply make it through from day to day, it is no wonder that such a plan brings along many problems, disillusion and pain. However, living our lives according to the great vision that is in line with God's plan for us, will see us shine, flourish and become a blessing to those around us.

"The glory of God is man fully alive; and to be alive consists in beholding God."
St. Irenaeus

I would love to hear from you.

Write to me at: derek@livethecallcoaching.com

CHAPTER 14: QUESTIONS 101
Diana Mascarenhas

Sometimes it is difficult to ask questions. It's hard to know who to ask and how to say it. In this chapter, we have put together lots of questions regarding life as Catholic Teens. If you have any questions of your own on faith or life as a Catholic teen, tweet them to: @AwakeCYM with the hashtag #Q101 or e-mail us at awakecym@gmail.com and your question may be answered anonymously in future editions of Essentials!

1. Why do I have to wait until marriage for sex?

That's like asking 'why do I have to wait until the water is hot for coffee?' We have become used to thinking of sex as a physical activity with no necessary relationship to marriage. But sex is essentially marital. We would be better off calling sex 'marital intercourse.' If you try and separate marital intercourse from marriage, you get neither. Or at least, you get a severely distorted and diminished version of one or the other. In Genesis 2:24 God spells out the right order: first you 'leave' your original family, then you 'cleave' to your spouse through the lifelong marriage vows, then you 'become' one flesh in marital intercourse.

2. What is abortion? Is it always wrong?

Abortion is the deliberate and direct destruction of an unborn human being — sometimes called an embryo or foetus. A human being begins to exist from the moment of conception. Because abortion is murder, it is always wrong. However, there are rare occasions where the death of an unborn child results as an unwanted side effect of some medical intervention to save the life of the mother. Because this is neither direct nor deliberate, it is usually not regarded as abortion. It is still a tragedy, nonetheless, and calls for compassion and pastoral support.

3. I feel embarrassed by my body, as everyone around me is much better looking than me. What should I do to feel better about myself?

One of the unique things about human beings, that distinguishes us from animals, is that we care deeply about other people's perceptions of us. This concern however can get out of hand and turn into an anxiety, and even a sickness. To get the balance right, we need to learn to view ourselves from God's perspective. He regards us with our bodies as wonderfully made, precious to Him and, despite our many failings, always worth loving and forgiving and calling to newness of life. Sin - our own and others' - distorts our self-perception, and can make us view our bodies and our sexuality with disgust or regret. But it is not our bodies that are to blame. Sin has its roots and deepest effects in the human heart and the will. It is here that God's healing power needs to flow. We can pray about our body image to God, knowing He will always listen to our prayers.

4. Why should I be 'pure' when people around me aren't? What does being 'pure' even mean?

One of our greatest temptations is to believe we are missing out on what others enjoy. This is the sin of envy, and it arises from thanklessness and a lack of trust in our heavenly Father's goodwill and generosity toward us. Purity is the experience of a good conscience before God, the joy of knowing that through Christ He has forgiven my sin, cleansed my heart, and withholds nothing that serves for my good and salvation. In this place of peace, I want to do nothing that displeases my Lord, upsets our friendship, or darkens my conscience. Only from this state of 'purity of heart', in which I rest in God's gaze of love and approval, can pure actions arise.

5. What does being a missionary mean? Do you have to go abroad for it?

The Great Commission given to us by Jesus Himself urges us to go out to all nations and make disciples. The encyclical Evangeli Nuntiandi (1975) states that the Church is missionary by nature. This means all the baptised are called to 'go out' to our work place, parishes, schools, universities and into the world we live in - first of all to proclaim that Jesus is Lord and secondly, to be witnesses through example. While some are called to leave their countries and set foot on foreign soil to sow the seeds of faith, we may be among those who never leave the shores of our nations just like St. Thérèse of Lisieux, patroness of Missions, who had a heart for the world through her prayer life, while living within the confines of her convent.

Pope Francis in his message for World Mission Day 2015 said "Mission is a passion for Jesus and a passion for his people". So let us first of all get to know Jesus.

6. Is everyone meant to be a missionary?

All Catholics are called to be missionary by virtue of their baptism. You and I are called to serve with joy and love in our hearts. It is the Holy Spirit that has been poured into our hearts and through the same Father whose love we all share and experience, we become children of God. "The laity (that's you and I) should cooperate in the Church's work of evangelisation as witnesses and at the same time, as living instruments, they share in her saving mission" (Ad Gentes, 41). So the answer is 'Yes', all of us are missionaries of God's love!

7. I keep being bullied at school for being a Christian. Sometimes I don't want to tell anyone I believe in God as people will bully me. What should I do?

Fear of rejection and alienation is a fear common to all young people. The need for love and acceptance is the greatest need in the life of a human person. We are often afraid of losing someone's friendship. Therefore, we allow others to dominate or control us and we would rather endure the suffering than be rejected or ridiculed. However, when we develop a living relationship with Christ, He reveals our true identity and we are no longer afraid of being who we are really called to be. We know we are accepted by Him and what is most important to us is that He loves and accepts us just the way we are.

8. None of my friends at school are Christians which is really tough, how can I be stronger standing up for my faith?

Perfect love casts out fear. When God's love fills our hearts, we are empowered to face all kinds of situations. Once we have found the 'pearl of great value' (Matthew 13:46), the inner man is made strong and we are able to become more than conquerors as Scripture says in Romans 8:37. The disciples of Jesus were timid men and two of them even betrayed Him. However, when the Holy Spirit of God came upon them at Pentecost, they were filled with courage and nothing could stop them from proclaiming the name of Jesus. A Christian who is filled with the Holy Spirit is fearless in the face of trials and persecution. Keep on praying for the Holy Spirit to inspire you!

9. Life at home is really difficult and it is hard to love my family. What can I do?

The three things we do not choose is the time of our birth and death and our family. Family is a reflection of the Trinitarian God we profess we believe in. The love relationship between the Father, Son and the Holy Spirit shows us the significance of a harmonious family bond.

There is no perfect family because of the brokenness in the

world today. God put each of us into a family and even if we have not received the love and nurture we were meant to experience, there was no other way God could have brought you into the world but through your parents. The only way we can embrace this plan is by praying for our families, and remembering that it on God that we first rely.

10. I feel peer-pressured into drinking, when is it wrong to drink?

Any sort of pressure is an indication that I am robbed of the freedom to make good choices for myself. When I drink because I want to be 'cool' like my friends or because I fear ridicule or scorn, then I am clearly under pressure. When I am not rooted in my identity and I fear I will lose my friendships, I would then go to any length to be accepted. God has given me a free will and once I know I am loved by Him and that I do not have to conform to other people's expectations of me, I will be truly free.

Secondly, if I am undergoing difficulties, challenges and failure and I find myself turning to alcohol as a form of escape, then I must know I am heading towards an addiction that will soon make me its slave. St. John of the Cross summed it up wonderfully when he said:

"If a man has a great love within Him, it's as if this love gives him wings, and he endures life's problems more easily,

because he has in himself that light which
is faith: to be loved by God and to let
oneself be loved by God in Christ Jesus."

CHAPTER 15: TESTIMONIES

Testimonies are a great way to share what God has done in each of our lives. We all have our story to tell. Whether it is a 'big or small' conversion, each of our stories are important to God and will speak to people. Whether we have been a Christian our whole lives, or if we converted and are the only Christian in our families, God can use each of our testimonies to lead others to Him.

Think of testimonies like this. Have you ever asked directions from someone to a café before? If they've been to the café, they know the road. They know which paths to take and which ones to avoid. They make a map come alive showing you the best route to take. So it is with testimonies. These are the stories of young people from around the world who have walked similar paths to you.

Bernadette

I was born and raised in Hong Kong to an interracial family, with a sister three years my junior. My mother, sister and I are all Catholic, and my father is Protestant. We all love going to the theatre, watching telly and travelling. Both my sister and I have always been Catholic, although this may have been more of a 'passive' thing rather than an 'active' thing until a few years ago. I have never doubted my faith, nor wished not to be a Catholic, but there were definitely times when I didn't act like a Christian or have an active Christian life aside from attending Mass every Sunday. There were, I'm ashamed to say, times where I was embarrassed about being a Catholic, and tried as best as I could to avoid Catholic gatherings/socials, or to avoid letting people know what my beliefs were.

A few years ago this changed. I'm not sure why, but one day my mother started to encourage my sister and I to pray more. The three of us started praying the Divine Mercy every day, we began going to Mass during the week, and I tried harder to listen more actively during the priests' homilies. I think it was the trip that my mum and her sister and mother took to the Holy Land a few months prior. I didn't go, for two reasons: first, my GCSEs were the following month, and second, my mother wanted me to go on the trip when I could fully understand and appreciate it all. At the time, I was dismissive of my mum's reasoning, but now, having really strengthened in my faith, I fully understand my mum's actions. Regardless of why my mother started to encourage us to be more active in our beliefs, my sister and I really grew in our faith in those few months, and I thank God for that every day, because I honestly do not know how I would have survived my dad's diagnosis with colon cancer otherwise.

My father's battle with cancer was definitely a challenging time for my family. It occupied most of my thoughts during a time where I had a lot of work to do at school and university applications to worry about. His illness put his work on hold for a while, and my mum had to take time off from her job as well to look after him as he went through his chemotherapy treatment. Despite all this, we really managed to hold together as a family, and I think that as a family, we have really come out from that time stronger. My father was admitted into a

Catholic hospital for both his surgery and his chemotherapy treatments. There were Nuns in this hospital who would visit the patients and spend time with them, as well as a chapel. One night, when I was spending the night by my dad's hospital bed, I decided to go visit this chapel. It was quiet - there was only one other person there - and I knelt down and prayed. It was that night when I realised how much my recent surge in faith had saved me.

My faith has even grown more since going to University. Upon joining the Catholic Society, I was, for the first time in my life, surrounded by people my age who also shared my beliefs and religion. This was very encouraging for me - it was confirmation (which I didn't need, but was nice to have anyway) that there were others like me who loved God as much as I do, facing the same challenges and struggles I do. It no longer felt like Catholicism was something that set me apart from people, and now my faith is something that I am very comfortable talking about with other people. Of course, I should never have been ashamed or embarrassed, but that's in the past now, and all I can do is try to be a better person, and trust in God to guide me through each day.

If I could ask you to take anything from what I have written, it would be this. Remember that you are not alone: not only are there many other young Catholics like you and I out there in the world, but God is always with us.

"Where can I go from your spirit?
Or where can I flee from your

presence?
If I ascend to heaven, you are there;
if I make my bed in Sheol,
you are there.
If I take the wings of the morning
and settle at the
farthest limits of the sea,
even there your hand shall lead me,
and your right hand shall hold me fast.

If I say, 'Surely the darkness
shall cover me,
and the light around me become night,'
even the darkness is not dark to you;
the night is as bright as the day,
for darkness is as light to you."
(Psalm 138:7-12 [139:7-12])

John

"And remember, I am with you always, to
the end of the age" (Matthew 28:20).

I don't have a radical change in lifestyle, or a near death experience that drastically altered my view of religion. I am a cradle Catholic, born and raised in the Catholic Church. I've gone to Mass every Sunday that I can remember. I could pray a Rosary in my sleep (no joke, I'm sure I have). In grade school my main out of school socializing was CCD (Confraternity of Christian Doctrine) and donuts after Sunday Mass. In high school I started to think about the priesthood, I even went to a special pre-seminary where high-school guys could prepare for the actual seminary. And I currently go to Franciscan university of Steubenville, one of the most charismatic Catholic Colleges in America.

I thank God for being raised in the faith. But that doesn't mean I've lived perfectly. There are certain aspects of my life that led me to doubt and confusion. The biggest problem I encountered was this: I never had to choose my faith as my own. Faith was always that thing that everyone around me was doing so I just went with it. Somewhere in junior year of high-school I started to realize that I wasn't completely convinced of my own faith. And it scared me. I decided by the end of the year that I was not going to be a priest. I had one more year of high-school to go and my doubts were not going away.

Around Christmas I started hanging out with this amazing girl. She was great. She was beautiful. And I was in love. After a couple months we started dating. Unfortunately I got caught in the mix of my emotions and doubts, and she and I started moving way too fast. We would stay out late, make out in the car, or sneak out in the early hours of the morning. Fortunately we never crossed the line completely, but we would constantly push that line. I could hear the voice of my conscience the further we went, but I kept quieting it because my faith was around me but not yet part of me.

Before she and I did anything too crazy I went off to college. Eventually the long distance wore on our relationship. I brought my situation to God, asked Him what she and I were supposed to do. That night He granted me a deep sense peace, like whatever happened with me and her was God's will. I took this feeling to mean things would work out. However a few days later she calls me, "John, we need to talk..." and that phone call broke my heart. It was also the last straw for my wavering faith. For several weeks I experienced the strongest doubts I have ever felt. There were a couple days where I didn't even think God existed. I begged him for a sign, but none came.

I was too blind with doubt and heartache to see at the time, but God was clearly speaking to me. Somehow even though I didn't really believe in Him, He drew me to Himself. Considering my state of mind and the doubts I was having, it made no sense whatsoever to run to God. But I felt this inexplicable urge that told me to go pray. While it was happening I attributed it to habit, but looking back I am convinced it was the Holy Spirit who was guiding me, because no habit could have made me pray at the time. I began seeing that prayer was more than just the sleeping Rosaries or routine grace before meals I had done before. The experience made me want to pray. And I have prayed nearly every night since.

Now that I am back, or mostly back, on my spiritual feet, I see God was walking with me throughout the whole series of events I just told you of, even from the first time I started pushing the limits of my conscience with this girl. God placed people in my life to guide me, events to show me his love, and even fire to strengthen my faith. One such person was my youth minister, Mark. Mark inspired me to serve and teach the faith to young people to lead by example and to pray in times of doubt. Mark and many others, who were placed in my life by God, helped me take the initial steps toward claiming my faith as my own. Events such as going to Christian summer conference with my friends inspired me to go to a strong Catholic College.

I found throughout my life that God is always willing to forgive you if you are willing to accept it. His love and mercy are endless and will be with you until the end of the age.

Therese

I am the eldest of five children, so I know a thing or two about the pressure of being a good role model to younger siblings. Being the eldest child also comes with a lot of responsibility. It usually means you get into a lot trouble especially when you have to cover for your sisters' or brothers' mistakes or when your siblings blame you for lots of things. I was born in India but moved to a little island between India and Africa on the equator called the Maldives. My family is very active in our faith. We go to Mass every Sunday, attend prayer meetings, sing in the church choir and every night say family prayer. The Maldives is a Muslim country, where the law prohibits anyone from practicing any other religion than Islam. If you were caught practicing another religion you would be deported. But my parents refused to give up their faith so we prayed in secret.

When I was seven, my parents decided to move to Australia so we could have a better life. Everything in Australia was different from home. I struggled to fit in at school and make friends. I was bullied because of my Indian accent. In an effort to stop the bulling I would spend hours practicing an

Australian accent but it made no difference. I was also bullied because of my faith, kids would call me names like "the Nun" and "Bible Freak." These names really hurt me. As I went to high school I started to hate being Christian because I saw many people who acted really holy in church but doing wrong things outside. I became like Peter in the gospel and pretended I didn't know who Jesus was so others would like me and accept me into their friendship circle. I started to live a double life, one that conformed to my friend's expectations at school and one that conformed to my parents' expectations at home.

One day my aunt gave me a book about a lady in the Bible called Esther (you can also find her story in the book called "Esther" in the Bible). I realised that I was a lot like Esther, I also hid the fact I was Christian so that people wouldn't hurt me. But unlike me, Esther was very brave. She was ready to face death to try and protect the people whom she loved. I realised that Esther didn't do it alone, she prayed for three whole days before she was given the strength to face her challenge. In the Bible it says:

"do not fear, for I am with you,
do not be afraid, for I am your God;
I will strengthen you, I will help you,
I will uphold you with my victorious right
hand" (Isaiah 41:10).

Esther was afraid but God gave her strength, I too was afraid but I knew that God would help me no matter what, because God loved me.

God loves you just as much as He loves me. **You see the fact you are breathing right now means that God is thinking about you.** If He stopped thinking about you, you wouldn't exist. I realised that God wasn't up in the clouds or in another galaxy, He is always right next to me and it's the same for you. "For nothing will be impossible with God" (Luke 1:37) and when you have Him with you, the things people say don't hurt so much. It is ok to be yourself as God is a perfect gentleman, He won't try to push in and take over, He just waits for you to ask and the joy that comes from knowing Him is like no other. So if you feel like you can't do something, always remember:

"I can do all things through him who strengthens me" (Philippians 4:13).

Catherine

When I was 17, I had my whole life planned out. I knew exactly where I wanted to go, how I wanted to get there, and no one was going to get in the way of my ambitions…Well, at least that's what I thought. Spring-time of my A-level year, everything seemed to go wrong in my life. I was rejected by all my Uni choices, at home my Mum fell ill, and tensions within the family meant I had no one to turn to. What little trust I may have had in God at that time was completely extinguished. I just felt a complete failure.

Although I was brought up in a Catholic family, I would only ever pray during that one hour of Mass each Sunday morning…and even that was difficult! It had never even occurred to me that I could speak to God anywhere at all. Yet, as all my ambitions fell away, and I started to really question what I wanted in life, I began to pray. For the first time in my life I spoke to God honestly. I told Him what a mess I was in, I told Him how frightened, angry and confused I felt, and I asked Him for help.

An opportunity came up for me to take a gap year at a Catholic Retreat centre. There I joined a team of young Catholics who taught me how truly alive the Church is, and how exciting faith can be! We worked with young people from all over the country who would come and spend a week with us learning about Christianity. For many it was their very first experience of faith. During that year I witnessed many miracles. Not of the dramatic, explosive kind, but of the healing that a person can experience when they realise how infinitely loved they are by their Creator. Through this, I too began to find freedom, from those insecurities and anxieties, from the thought that I was a failure.

One of the highlights of the year for me came right at the start. Pope Benedict XVI visited the UK in September 2010, and we were lucky enough to travel down to London as a team to see him. In his address to young people, the Pope spoke some words which I will never forget.

"I ask you to look into your hearts, each
day, to find the source of all true love.
Jesus is always there,
quietly waiting for us to be still with Him
and to hear His voice."

I realised that I had spent so much time stressing out about making big decisions, but had never stopped to reflect about the more important things, about what my life might actually be about.

Pope Benedict went on to say:

"Even amidst the busyness
and stress of our daily lives
we need to make space for silence,
because it is in silence that we find God.
And in silence that we
discover our true self."

And so I realised, just because my plans hadn't worked out, it didn't mean that I had failed. It just meant that He who created me, He who knows me better than I know myself, had bigger and better things in mind.

From that day on, I decided to try and make a little more time each day for silence. Of course, that's easier said than done! Anyone who knows me knows that I am not a very silent person. But, like in any friendship, our relationship with God works both ways. Sure it's great to talk (and talk a lot, in my case!), but no friendship can possibly work out if we don't also take the time to listen! Of course, the Lord doesn't 'speak' very loudly…in fact, most people have never heard his voice! But, as Scripture says: "What no eye has seen, nor ear heard, nor the human heart conceived, what God has prepared for those who love him" (1 Corinthians 2:9).

Silence is essential. I mean, we're not talking anything too big here, no one would expect you to become a hermit! But even just 5 minutes of quiet each day can make a huge difference. As soon as I started to take this time out, and as soon as I tried to recognise the presence of God in every aspect of my day-to-day life, everything changed. I began to see life not as something to be scared of, but as an adventure to be embraced!

In every heartbeat, Jesus is there waiting for us to respond, waiting for us to acknowledge His love. "In him we live and move and have our being" (Acts 17:28). So, no matter what the future holds, whatever difficulties we may face, we are never alone. God, who created us, who loves us and who dwells within us, has a plan for each one of us.

Now I am in my 3rd year at University and, honestly, I have no clue what the future holds. But the difference is now I know who holds my future, and if I continue to walk with Him, I am certain He will lead me to eternal happiness.

Matthew

My name is Matthew and I am the youngest of two

children. I'm dyslexic and have ADD (Attention Deficit Disorder). Both my parents are Catholic therefore I was brought up in a Catholic home, being a practicing Catholic and going to Mass every Sunday just to fulfill my weekly duties. I didn't really understand Mass and was forced to go just because my parents went. My parents were very strong Catholics and my dad was very involved in the church and so was my mum since I was very young.

When I was growing up I had a lot of problems studying as the dyslexia made it very hard for me to study especially reading and writing. A simple piece of work would take me two times longer than for others to do and this would irritate me and I would compare myself with other people who got better results. I hated that I could not achieve like the rest when I did so much work but didn't do as well. This is a big deal being in Asia where your worth is based on how well you perform.

To add to it, when I was 16 my dad was diagnosed with Parkinson's which is a nerve disease that cannot be cured. Medication can only slow down the process of him getting worse. As time passed the medication he had to take was getting stronger and stronger at different stages of his disease. When I was 18 my father's condition kept getting worse and worse to the point that he had to take really strong medication that had side effects of hallucination, depression and paranoia. Due to being under the influence of the drug, he would think I was fighting with my neighbors and would wake me up from sleep at three in the morning and scold me. He would not talk to my mum or sister because he thought that they were against him so therefore the only person he would listen to would be me. So I had to be with him all the time so I didn't have time to spend with my friends or do anything I wanted to do. Being slow in my studies and not being able to study much meant my grades were falling and my dad would scold me. I understood but what made me sad was my mum would join in when I expected her to at least understand since she knew what I went through.

I got very angry with God for giving me so many problems to deal with and this caused me to question who is God and how He could let my dad go through this disease, especially as he was someone that did so much for God in the Church and brought me and my sister up as Catholics. Since then I started not to want to go to Mass but my parents would nag me and I would not hear the end of it if I didn't go. So therefore I would go and not pay attention.

Soon, since all my time had to be focused on my dad, and the only way I could escape from being in the house and taking care of my dad was for me to go and do church activities. Since that's the only thing that my parents would let me go for, I took the opportunity to help in my local college ministry at my church and I also quickly took up a leader post that demanded more time of me in church, just to be more out of the house and help out in camps. Everyone in ministry would praise me for always wanting to help in every project and would think that I am very holy.

Another escape route from the house would be if I had an educational project to do. I would also use excuses like having group projects for my university to do at a friend's house and I would go and spend time in the clubs and parties with friends, getting drunk and stoned on drugs.

By doing this I was living a double life. I was one person at home and in church and another when I was with my friends. In church I was a leader involved in youth ministry and on the other hand I was out partying, drinking and smoking in the clubs.

In one camp that I helped out, at I met a facilitator that I knew in my younger teens, and he drifted away from the church once and recently came back to the Lord. He told me his life story and conversion. He went through the same things I was going through and worse. He has been into drugs and alcohol and he challenged me to give God a chance to show Himself to me. That night I challenged God to show Himself to me, if He really was a God of love. I shouted and finally let go of my true emotion that I was carrying and that night I cried at Jesus' feet asking Him to take control of my life. Then he showed me how much He loved me by giving me this peace beyond words, a peace that nothing or no one could have given.

Since then my faith journey has been growing slowly but surely improving. There are sometimes when I fall but I know my God loves me and will lift me up every time. I started wanting to gain knowledge about the faith, learning how great it is to be part of a religion with rich history. God has shown me how my past and what I have been through is being used for His glory and how I am able to talk with youth that have family issues and help them.

With that came the call to serve Him and share with

people what He has done for me. I took the step to answer that call by serving Him in His vineyard. I felt the Lord asking me to go to be His light and salt of the earth by being a missionary in New Zealand.

So if anyone is questioning the existence of God, or even if God is so great why does He let us suffer, I would encourage them to challenge God to show Himself to you like I did, and I promise you that He will take up your challenge and show you a whole new world.

Benedict

We all come to Christ in different ways. Ask any young Catholic how they came by their faith and I guarantee you'll get a unique story every time. Some of us have the good fortune to be raised in a Catholic family, with unique role models like mothers or brothers. Some find faith through a personal spiritual experience, a 'lightning bolt' moment in which they suddenly see the light. Others dive into theology and doctrine, seeking truth, and are overwhelmed by what they find in the pages of Scripture and Church teaching. Everyone's path has its own flavour, personal stories that develop into individual relationships with God.

I personally hopped around on a bunch of paths before I realized the destination. I was given every opportunity imaginable to really commit to my faith, but it took years to do it.

Technically, I was raised as a Catholic, in a Catholic

family. But it was a pretty halfhearted Catholicism which my family practiced. We missed Mass often, almost never went to Confession, and didn't really engage much with our local parish. It's not that my parents weren't passionate believers; they just didn't really make the practice of their faith a priority. I was more or less the same way.

Sure, I prayed occasionally. And when I asked God to work changes in my life, my prayers were always answered. I did well in school, started a relationship with a great girl, had a close circle of friends. But I always vainly attributed those developments to my own awesomeness, not realising that God was calling out to me, "Look how much I love you, look how much I give to you, come back to me."

"Listen! I am standing at the door, knocking; if you hear my voice and open the door, I will come in to you and eat with you, and you with me" (Revelations 3:20).

So the path of family and the path of prayer were both laid at my feet, but I was blind and kept stumbling around in my own ignorance. I didn't give God a second thought, even as I entered high school. Just as my own pressures were building, my family life began to disintegrate and my parents' marriage became increasingly strained. Despite all God had given me, the most consideration I ever gave Him was a vague sense that He had abandoned me by allowing these bad things to build up.

When I was 16 years old, however, I was invited to a Catholic Bible study group hosted by my girlfriend's mother. I agreed to go along, not so much because I wanted to learn about the Word of God, but because I wanted to make my girlfriend happy and maybe do a little sucking up to her family as well. What I learned there changed my life utterly.

"Jesus answered, 'You do not know now
what I am doing, but later you will
understand'" (John 13:7).

I found so much truth in the words of Scripture. Reading the story of salvation, book by book, swept away all my indifference and cynicism towards the Christian message. Of course, I had heard the words before, but now I really understood what they meant, how it all fit together. It's difficult for me even to explain how profoundly this affected me. The best analogy I can give (though I'm actually stealing it from the Bible) is that of a sudden fire blazing up inside me, burning out all the doubts and skepticism that were weighing me down.

"Is not my word like fire, says the LORD,
and like a hammer
that breaks a rock in pieces?"
(Jeremiah 23:29)

Abraham's faith, David's sins and forgiveness, Job's suffering, the Gospel in all its glory, the humanity of St. Peter, the fervor of St. Paul. Before, they were only stories. But something about that Bible study made them come alive in me, made them as deeply personal as if I were reading about myself. And each story seemed to play on the others, each verse held a deep significance. Everything about the Old Testament emphatically pointed forward to the Gospel, everything about the New Testament emphatically pointed back to the Gospel, and through all that pointing, I could see the Church.

I was always taught by my secular colleagues and teachers that there was a great battle between religion and science, that the Bible contradicted reality. I was always told by my Protestant friends that the Catholic Church was incompatible with Scripture, that the Eucharist was purely symbolic. I was always assured that nobody actually believed the Church's teachings on marriage, sexuality, and abortion, that none of it was really in the Bible, anyways. The sheer magnitude of how wrong all these assumptions were just blew my mind. I remember leaving each meeting of the Bible study shaking my head in wonder, amazed by how perfectly everything in that Book worked together and how much I could still learn.

It was then that I found something I didn't really know I was looking for. Peace. For so long, unhappiness, cynicism, and anxiety had been eating away at me from the inside and I didn't even realize it. Diving in to the Word of God and the theological foundations of the Catholic Church brought peace, in a way that my family and my own halfhearted attempts at prayer never did. It was like being freed from chains, or letting go of a heavy load, or any of the other clichés. And it remains the greatest feeling I have ever experienced.

"I have said this to you, so that in me you
may have peace" (John 16:33).

Maintaining that peace in the world I lived in, of course, was no easy task. All around me were people who couldn't even imagine the revelation I had been given, people who were content to behave immorally, people who looked down with contempt on us simple-minded fools who still believed in things like 'right' and 'wrong.' The pressure to give in to the temptations those people offered was, and is, intense. At times, I didn't think I was strong enough, and I was right. But God was strong enough for both of us and He guarded that inner peace within me.

My journey to Christ was not through family or prayer or even dramatic spiritual conversion, but rather through the study of the Bible and Catholic theology. Now, that may seem dull to most people, and I don't blame them. But the point is not that intense study is the only way to reach the Catholic truth. The point is that the roads to Christ are many and varied, and just because one or two don't work out at first does not mean that the destination is unreachable. If you're reading these stories and thinking "Why hasn't that happened to me?" or "I tried that and I didn't feel anything," don't give up. God is there, waiting for you, and if you're patient and sincere in trying to find Him, He'll lay the path in front of you.

"When you search for me, you will find
me; if you seek me with all your heart"
(Jeremiah 29:13).

Maria

Christ's movements in my life have always been most
visible to me through friendships and relationships. Having
been brought up a Catholic and having quite dedicated
Catholics on both sides of the family meant that I was used to
going to Mass and calling myself a Christian but not really
thinking much more about it. I became aware of God's
presence and action in the world, and specifically in my life,
through friendship with a community of non-Catholic
Christians in Afghanistan, where I was living at the time with
my family. The Christians I met there were not all missionaries
but many believed in giving their lives to help others and just
by getting to know them better, I realised what an important
role God played in their lives.

For me, a most memorable quote from a good friend's
mother in response to my question about how much longer
they would be living in Afghanistan was, "I don't know, it's
God's choice". Not only in their lifestyles where these people
glorifying the Lord, but also in their worship. Worship, during
the services we would attend at the end of week, was a way for
me to get close to Christ, to praise him, to show how much I
loved Him by how loud I could sing and to think about how
the words in the songs were visible in my own life. Worship

also made me feel part of that community of Christians from all different denominations and walks of life and was one of the only ways I knew to pray.

Just before my 14th birthday, I had to move back to England and lived with my grandparents while the rest of my family remained scattered around the world. The change was difficult, not so much because I missed my family but because I found the new culture extremely difficult to adapt to. Although I was at a Catholic school, none of the people I met were interested in their faith. I missed my friends a lot, I missed talking about religion and I felt that no one really understood me. At that time, my family decided that it would be good for me to do my First Communion as, living in Afghanistan, I hadn't really had a chance. This, combined with being Confirmed a year later, kept me on journey of learning about Christ and His Church. I learnt to love the more 'traditional' worship of my parish Church but started learning the guitar so I could play all those brilliant songs from my Afghanistan days.

I decided to change schools for 6th form and ended up going to a boarding school run alongside a community of monks. My closest friends from those school days were all people who understood how important my faith was to me. The way I used to describe it was that because my faith is such a big part of who I am, if you can understand it, than you can know me better. In my last year at school, I became friends with a group of Chileans who used to come to our school to work in the Chaplaincy and they invited me to spend my gap year working for their movement in Chile. They completely understood what I said about friendship and faith and told me that **friendships based in Christ are the deepest friendships of all**. I decided to take the leap of faith and head out to Chile the year after school because I realised that with this movement, I would be able to learn more about God and more about myself. Since God is in the deepest part of who I am, I figured it would help me understand more of what my life was about. At the time, I had a lot of questions about the meaning of life and how I was supposed to give it all to God and to "not worry about your life, [and] what you will eat" (Matthew 6:25). This was what I was struggling with, but I knew that as long as I kept moving towards knowing Christ better and seeing what He was doing in my life, then I would find the answer.

At that point, when I was about 18 and had just finished school and was about to start a gap year, I could look back on my life and say that I had never had a 'conversion' moment that people talk about, a moment when they had a vision or heard Christ speak to them and so on. All I could see were all the blessings I had received, how much love and joy there was in my life. Also, I could see so many decisions that I had made along the way, or situations when I had really prayed to see the way that had brought me to where I was now, a place that I was so happy to be in, and I knew that God was guiding me.

Writing this now, I am still trying to answer those questions and I am still searching for God but I have already learnt so much along the way. I am full of hope for the future because although the way is not always clear, for "I can do all things through him who strengthens me" (Philippians 4:13).

I still sing, a lot, because it reminds me of how good the

Lord is and helps me channel the feelings I have towards Him! I read my Bible (not as much as I should but at least every day) because that is the place where I encounter Christ and can listen to him talking directly to me and, very importantly, I try to love the people I am with, my friends, my family, my classmates, the people who make up my community in fact, through serving them and recognising that God is in them too.

CHAPTER 16: BEYOND ESSENTIALS

Being a Catholic teen is one of the greatest blessings we can ever have. You and I are fully equipped, able to do all things through Christ who gives us strength, to achieve great things in our world. Let no one ever speak down to you, let no one dismiss you because you are young. We are called to be Saints. We are called to great things, and God is with us every step of the way. Dream big dreams. Every dream in our heart has been placed there by God, and He will never ask of us anything which we cannot achieve. So let's dream big together! God is alive and active in our lives, even when we don't feel it. As a young person, we have such an incredible privilege to spend time with people from all levels society at school and university. Let's be a witness to the One who loved us into existence! Will you pray with me?

Heavenly Father, my Creator and
Provider, let your will be done in my life.

Jesus, my Saviour, you are the Way, the
Truth and the Life. Be my peace in the
midst of the storm, and my Light when I
can't see the path.

Holy Spirit, come with Your power and
healing. Be the fire burning in my heart
and be my courage when I feel scared.

Lord God, thank you that you love me,
you care for me and that you have a plan
for my life. I choose today to live for you,
and I invite you into my life as my Lord

and Saviour.

Mary, my mother and the Mother of Jesus,
please pray for me as I walk the path to
Sainthood that God is calling me to.

May God be praised every day of my life.
In Jesus' Name,

Amen!

Made in the USA
San Bernardino, CA
19 November 2017